KU-741-818

ESSENTIAL
MARRAKECH

Written by Jane Egginton

© Automobile Association Developments Limited 2009
First published 2009

ISBN: 978-0-7495-5980-9

Published by AA Publishing, a trading name of Automobile Association Developments Limited, whose registered office is Fanum House, Basing View, Basingstoke, Hampshire RG21 4EA.
Registered number 1878835.

Colour separation: MRM Graphics Ltd
Printed and bound in Italy by Printer Trento S.r.l.

A03606
Maps in this title produced from map data supplied by:
   Global Mapping, Brackley, UK (www.globalmapping.uk.com) Copyright ©Global Mapping/Kartographie Huber/The XYZ Digital Map Company
   Source: *Marrakech, Cartoville Gallimard* ©Gallimard Loisirs 2008

About this book

This book is divided into six sections.

The essence of Marrakech pages 6–19 Introduction; Features; Food and Drink; Short Break including the 10 Essentials

Planning pages 20–33
Before You Go; Getting There; Getting Around; Being There

Best places to see pages 34–55
The unmissable highlights of any visit to Marrakech

Best things to do pages 56–71
Great cafés; stunning views and more

Exploring pages 72–129
The best places to visit in Marrakech, organized by area

Excursions pages 130–152
Places to visit out of town

Maps

All map references are to the maps on the covers. For example, Bab Agnaou has the reference ➕ 2a – indicating the grid square in which it is to be found

Admission prices

An indication of costs is given by € signs: €€€ denotes higher prices, €€ denotes average prices, € denotes lower prices

Hotel prices

Price are per room per night:
€ budget (under 1,200Dh);
€€ moderate (1,200Dh–2,300Dh);
€€€ expensive to luxury (over 2,300Dh)

Restaurant prices

Price for a three-course meal per person without drinks: € budget (under 230Dh); €€ moderate (230Dh–464Dh); €€€ expensive (over 464Dh)

Contents

The essence of...

Marrakech is exotic and hypnotic: an ancient desert trading post and indulgent travel destination. The chaotic medina at its heart is utterly medieval, yet the extravagant tourist developments of the New City are straight out of the 21st century. There is fine architecture in delightful palaces and gardens, whose pools cool the city's sultry heat. Art galleries and cultural centres counterpoint the decadence of French cafes and exquisite luxury hotels, while the haunting call to prayer adds spiritual weight and the snow-capped peaks of the legendary Atlas Mountains provide a continuous dramatic backdrop.

THE ESSENCE OF MARRAKECH

Don't let Marrakech's proximity to Europe fool you. Initially overwhelming, with dizzying alleyways and few conventional sights, Marrakech is a city to take your time over. Your holiday memories will be of a belly dancer on your restaurant table, of sipping mint tea in the depths of the souks, of sinking into the pool of your stylish hotel after a day on the dusty, donkey-laden streets of the medina…

LANDSCAPE

Marrakech's immediate geography is simply extraordinary. From the main square, on the hottest day, when the snakes and shoppers are slithering to a halt under the stultifying heat, you can still see the snow on the Atlas Mountains. They, along with the empty red expanse of the desert and the cool breeze of the Atlantic Ocean are all within reach of the city.

PEOPLE

Marrakeshis are Arabs, but also Berbers – the original inhabitants from the mountains – as well as French expats.

Generally they are kind, warm, funny people; take time to engage with the cleaner or cook at your hotel, your masseur, even the shopkeepers in the souk.

● The average wage in Morocco is around €10 a day.
● 50 per cent of the population are under 20.
● The penetrating call to prayer occurs five times a day – the first at 4am.

RIADS

Riads (courtyard hotels) provide sanctuary and even sanity in the mayhem of the medina. Invariably infused with the personality of their (frequently European) owners, many offer an exquisite experience, with hammam (Turkish bath) facilities and -personal service that may well be the highlight of any trip.

THE FUTURE

Thanks partly to a law that nothing can be built higher than the Koutoubia Mosque, Marrakech is growing outwards instead of upwards – with major development fuelled by massive foreign investment. Having barely shaken off French colonialism, foreign influence is once more shaping the city, with millions of dollars of inward investment creating a property explosion.

● 'Vision 2010' is the young King's ambitious aim to increase tourism to a staggering 10 million visitors to Morocco per year.
● 13 more casinos, more than 100 enormous international hotels and several new golf courses are currently being built around Marrakech.
● Unemployment in Marrakech is around 10 per cent and illiteracy at 40 per cent. Although the development projects aim to spur growth, it is uncertain to what extent individuals and local communities will profit.

The 'open skies' policy ending all restrictions on flights from the EU has already brought in huge numbers of tourists on budget airlines. Now the rattling Marrakech Express of 1960s fame is to be replaced with a futuristic high-speed rail link direct from Paris.

food & drink

Morocco is the Queen of North African cuisine and her food has been exported to some of the best restaurants around the world. Moroccan cook books are devoured internationally and now a new breed of chefs – many of them French with Michelin stars – are bringing haute cuisine to the city of Marrakech.

TIME

Time is the essence of traditional Moroccan meals. Cooks have used the same recipes for centuries. The rich, delicate flavours are the result of slow cooking, and a true Moroccan feast should be lingered over for hours.

MELTING POT

Moroccan food is a direct result of its cultural influences and Marrakech – as an ancient centre for trade – is its culinary core. French colonialism lingers in sophisticated dishes; while the staples

of couscous, *tagines* (the stew and the traditional cooking pots in which they are cooked) and *harira* (spicy garlic, chickpea and tomato soup) are testament to Berber origins. The nomads brought dates, milk and bread, while the Andalusian influence from nearby Spain can be tasted in lemons, olives and olive oil. From the east, the Arabs introduced saffron, coriander, cumin and paprika.

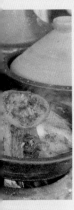

KIF-KIF (SAME SAME)

Set meals – invariably salads, pigeon *pastilla* (pie), tagine with couscous and Moroccan pastries – are annoyingly the only option in many tourist restaurants. Intended to resemble a Moroccan feast, visitors can find it drawn-out, expensive and a rather unsatisfying experience. While a few of the best can be a good approximation of a real feast, once on a single trip to Marrakech is enough for most visitors. À la carte Moroccan, Asian and international restaurants can all be found too, and have been detailed in this guide.

HOME-COOKED CUISINE

Try to eat at least once in a riad – they generally offer family-style cooking that is much better than restaurant food. Many are open to non-guests, but in all cases reservations should be made a day in advance. Many riads also offer small, casual cookery classes that are highly recommended.

SMALL PLATES

A Moroccan salad is a varied and vegetarian delight of jewel-like colours, usually served as a starter. Non meat-eaters don't have an easy time of it, but

harira soup is sometimes cooked without meat stock, there are international restaurants and omelettes and pizzas can be found in many cafes and restaurants in the city.

SWEET TEETH
Moroccans love their sweet dishes – rich, even cloying, combinations of honey-soaked pastries, laced with cinnamon –

and Marrakech, particularly the New City, is dotted with patisseries.

MUSLIM WHISKEY
Moroccans joke that their sweet mint tea, which they drink throughout the day, is 'Muslim Whiskey'. While Islam forbids alcohol, it is possible to drink beers, fine wine and cocktails as long as it is not in sight of a mosque.

short break

If you only have a short time to visit Marrakech and would like to take home some unforgettable memories, the following suggestions will give you a wide range of sights and experiences that won't take very long, won't cost very much and will remain with you long after you have returned home.

● **Absorb the atmosphere** of Jemaa El Fna, a UNESCO site and a seething mass of humanity (➤ 78).

● **Get lost in the souks** of the Northern Medina, shopping for souvenirs (➤ 52).

● **Steam yourself** in a hammam – a traditional spa, where you can get massaged and scrubbed, hotel hammams are open to non-residents.

● **Take a horse drawn carriage** around the pink city walls and gates (➤ 29).

● **Admire the magnificence of the** Koutoubia Mosque with its landmark spire and golden globes (➤ 42).

مدرسة ابن يوسف
MEDERSA BEN YOUSSEF

● **Eat at the enormous outdoor dining area** of the Night Market, tucking into spicy sausages and sustaining bowls of soup (➤ 48).

● **Retreat to the cool oasis** of the Majorelle Gardens, with their soothing cobalt blue walls and towering palms (➤ 38).

● **Marvel at the scale** of the once splendid Badii Palace (➤ 50).

● **Enjoy the serene architecture** of Ben Youssef (➤ 44).

● **Escape the heat of the city** in the snowy Atlas Mountains (➤ 134), or at Essaouira on the breezy Atlantic coast (➤ 142).

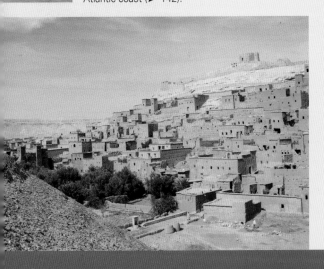

Planning

Before you go

WHEN TO GO

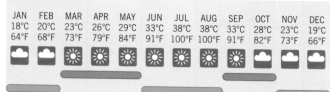

JAN	FEB	MAR	APR	MAY	JUN	JUL	AUG	SEP	OCT	NOV	DEC
18°C	20°C	23°C	26°C	29°C	33°C	38°C	38°C	33°C	28°C	23°C	19°C
64°F	68°F	73°F	79°F	84°F	91°F	100°F	100°F	91°F	82°F	73°F	66°F

🔵 High season   ⬤ Low season

Rainfall is very low in Marrakech but when a winter downpour comes, the streets do get muddy. The summer months are unbearably hot, although Essaouira and the Atlas mountains are cooler. The temperatures shown are the average daily maximum for each month.

As well weather conditions, cultural and religious events may influence when you visit. Christmas, New Year and Easter are the busy times – rooms get booked far in advance, and prices rise significantly. The holy month of Ramadan (What's on When ➤ 24) is a movable feast, around 11 days earlier each successive year in the Western calendar. During Ramadan you may find irregular opening and closing times as the Islamic people observe their faith.

WHAT YOU NEED

● Required
○ Suggested
▲ Not required

Ensure your passport is stamped on arrival. A missing stamp can cause problems with Passport Control on your departure. The requirements below apply to visits of three months or less.

	UK	Germany	USA	Netherlands	Spain
Passport (valid for 6 months)	●	●	●	●	●
Visa (regulations can change – check before journey)	▲	▲	▲	▲	▲
Onward or Return Ticket	▲	▲	▲	▲	▲
Health Inoculations	▲	▲	▲	▲	▲
Health Documentation (➤ 23, Health Insurance)	○	○	○	○	○
Travel Insurance	○	○	○	○	○
Driving Licence (National or International)	●	●	●	●	●
Car Insurance Certificate (if own car)	●	●	●	●	●
Car Registration Document (if own car)	●	●	●	●	●

WEBSITES

Moroccan Tourist Board
www.visitmorocco.com

I Love Marrakesh
www.ilove-marrakesh.com

TOURIST OFFICES AT HOME

In the UK

Moroccan National Tourist Office
205 Regent Street, 2nd Floor
London W1R 7DE
☏ (020) 7437 0073
www.visitmorocco.org

In the USA

Moroccan Tourist Office
20 East 46th St., Suite 1201
New York, NY 10017

☏ 212/557-2520
www.tourism-in-morocco.com

In Canada

Moroccan National Tourist Office
Suite 1460, 2001 Rue Université
Montreal, Quebec H3A 2A6
☏ 514/842-8111/2

TRAVEL AND HEALTH INSURANCE

Make sure your travel insurance package includes a minimum of
£2 million towards medical treatment, including provision to fly you
home in the case of an emergency. If you go abroad twice or more
each year, an annual travel insurance policy might be the best value.
Don't rely on the inclusive insurance provided with credit cards, as this
very rarely provides sufficient cover.

TIME DIFFERENCES

| GMT 12 noon | Marrakech 12 noon | Germany 1PM | USA (NY) 7AM | Netherlands 1PM | Spain 1PM |

Marrakech local time is GMT (as London) but the clocks do not go
forward in summer. From March to October, the city is one hour
behind London and four hours ahead of New York.

NATIONAL HOLIDAYS

1 Jan *New Year's Day*
11 Jan *Manifesto of Independence*
9 Mar *Aïd al-Mawlid*
(Prophet's Birthday)
1 May *Labour Day*
30 Jul *Feast of the Throne*
14 Aug *Fête Oued Eddahab*
(Oued Eddahab Allegiance Day)
20 Aug *Révolution du Roi et du Peuple*
(The King and the People's
Revolution Day)

21 Aug *King Mohamed's Birthday*
21 Sep *Aïd al-Fitr*
(End of Ramadan – moveable).
6 Nov *Marche Verte*
(Anniversary of the Green March)
18 Nov *Fête de l'Indépendence*
(Independence Day)
28 Nov *Aïd al-Adha*
(Feast of the Sacrifice – moveable).
18 Dec *Fatih Muharram*
(Islamic New Year – moveable).

* Some of Morocco's national holidays are based on the Islamic Lunar Calendar. Dates for these events (asterisked) are given for the Western year of 2009, but will be around 11 days earlier each subsequent year.

WHAT'S ON WHEN

Pick up the free monthly entertainment guide, *Marrakech Pocket* (www.marrakechpocket.com) from shops and hotels. Although all in French, it's easy enough to spot the latest art exhibitions, cultural events, bar openings etc.

January *Marrakech International Marathon*: Great athletes from all over the world mix with locals and charity runners (www.marathon-marrakech.com).
February *Dakka Marrakchia Festival*, Marrakech: A new five-day festival aimed at reviving a 1000 year-old tradition. Local musicians from the city's seven districts perform percussive musical tributes to the ancient spiritual guardians.
May *Alizés Musical Spring Festival*, Essaouira: Four days of music bring together orchestral performances, chamber music and opera (www.alizesfestival.com).
June *Festival of Gnawa and World Music*, Essaouira: The seaside town is a great setting, the music is uplifting and interesting, and the crowds are friendly (www.festival-gnaoua.co.ma). The fun goes on around the town for five days.

July *Marrakech Popular Arts Festival*: Musicians, dancers, and acrobats from all over Morocco and beyond, with performers taking over prestigious venues across the city.

August *Imilchil Marriage Feast*, High Atlas: Berber tradition in which elaborate public courtships lead up a day of multiple weddings. Music, dance and a bustling market attract many curious visitors.

September/ October *Ramadan*: The sacred month of Islam means daily fasting, and special attention to the Koran's teachings. Non-Muslim visitors to Marrakech should make particular efforts not to cause offence. Don't smoke or eat in the street before sunset, don't use bad language, and dress modestly (men and women).

October *Festival of the Atlantic Andalusias*, Essaouira: A mainly musical affair, with some art and dance events, celebrating the Andalusian contribution 0to the cultures of Spain, South America and Africa.

November/December *International Film Festival*, Jemaa El Fna: Showcasing world cinema, the festival attracts artsy crowds and stars too. The open air screenings are great fun in the evening (www.festivalmarrakech.net).

Getting there

BY AIR

Marrakech, Menara Airport

6km (3.7 miles) to city centre

🚆 N/A

🚌 No.11 or No. 19 every 30 minutes

🚗 15 minutes

For full-service flights from the UK and continental Europe, look at Iberia (www.iberia.com) and the national airline Royal Air Maroc (www.royalairmaroc.com). RAM also flies from New York, stopping off in Casablanca, and their no-frills subsidiary Atlas Blue (www.atlas-blue.com) flies direct to Marrakech from many European hubs. Other European budget options include Easyjet (www.easyjet.com), Ryanair (www.ryanair.com), Thomsonfly (www.thomsonfly.com), Jet4You (www.jet4you.com) and TUI (www.tuifly.com).

FROM MENARA AIRPORT

It is well worth having your riad or hotel pre-arrange a transfer from the airport. You probably won't pay any more than if you try to negotiate on arrival as the taxi drivers operate something of a cartel. Best of all, the driver will reach your destination with the minimum of fuss.

ARRIVING BY RAIL

A rail journey from Europe will take you south to the Spanish port of Algeciras and after the ferry crossing to Tangier (www.trasmediterranea.es), south again to Marrakech with ONCF railways (www.oncf.ma). To plan your route from a European capital, visit www.seat61.com. Inter-rail cards (for those under 26 years of age) are valid for use in Morocco.

ARRIVING BY BUS

Eurolines (www.eurolines.co.uk) operate services form mainland Europe and Britain to Marrakech, and to Essaouira. You will be on the bus for at least two days.

Getting around

IN THE MEDINA

Walking Meandering around the ancient medina, you might feel almost perpetually lost, but this is all part of the fun. With twisting narrow alleyways and confusingly similar intersections, a compass might come in handy, but many prefer to wander aimlessly and be surprised by the city's delights. Those with young children may prefer to avoid the medina on foot, with its buzzing scooters and plodding donkeys, uneven walkways and often searing heat. Older children, ten and older, tend to appreciate the medieval feel

and strange sights, smells and sounds. The medina is encircled by the old city walls. Walking beyond the walls is like hiking along the side of a dusty motorway and there are few concessions to pedestrians.

Hustlers Avoid the boys and young men who approach you in the street to assist with directions. Although almost certainly harmless, they will want to charge you for directions or guidance and might waste your time with a painful detour to their 'uncle's shop'. If you do get lost, don't panic and don't wander around looking desperate. Ask a shopkeeper, or pick out a local who is not obviously vying for your attention, and ask them to help.

Guides In the past, a guide would most certainly have been a good idea, if simply to keep the hustlers off your back. However, police crackdowns have now made this largely unnecessary. If you do want a guide, get your hotel to recommend one, or get a licensed guide from the tourist office. Always agree a price beforehand and be aware that they may get hefty commissions from certain shops.

PUBLIC TRANSPORT

Buses With taxis abundant and cheap, few travellers use public transport, but for those on a budget, or eager to plunge into local life, there is a public bus system. Do watch out for pickpockets. Bus number1 will take you to Guéliz in the New City. The number 8 runs to the train station, the number 10 to the coach station, while the number 11 heads south west to the airport, stopping at the Ménara Gardens.

TAXIS

Always agree a price first, as most drivers refuse to use their meters with tourists. Before you depart, ensure the driver clearly understands your destination and don't be afraid to get out immediately if it looks like he has no idea where you want to go.

Grand taxis These are bigger cars, usually Mercedes, and serve as collective taxis for up to five people. They are not much use if you are going deep into the old town, as they are limited to the big streets at the edge of the medina but for a group of four people, these are often better value than two petit taxis and they are a better alternative to rental cars for longer journeys out of the city.

Petit taxis These are small yellow hatch-backs with meters, though you will often have to agree a price due to 'a broken meter'. It is cheaper to hail one in the street than from a hotel or restaurant, although the doorman will often communicate your destination better than you can. Even petit taxis will only get you so far in the medina, so be prepared to do a bit of walking, and do remember: the petit taxis can take no more than three passengers per car.

CALÈCHES

These open horse-drawn carriages are great if you want to soak up th
sights and sounds of Marrakech on the move. Agree a price for your
journey in advance and don't expect to get anywhere in a hurry. They
also be rented by the hour (around 90dh per hour) for sight-seeing. H
to the Calèche stand at Place de la Foucauld, just beyond the south v
corner of Jemaa El Fna.

TOUR BUSES

A red double-decker bus is a strange sight around the medina and on
you certainly can't fail to spot. Although more of a tour than public
transport, the 24-hour hop-on hop-off ticket makes this a useful way
for newcomers to get their bearings, particularly with the multi-lingua
recorded information system.

The buses operate two different routes. 'Marrakech Monumental'
the Theatre Royal, Palais des Congres, Place de la Liberte and Saadie
tombs, while the 'Romantique' route takes in Les Jardin Majorelle, Le
Tikida Garden and Palmeraie Golf Palace. A recorded audio system
provides tour highlights in any of eight languages, with the last bus
running in the early evening most days.

CAR RENTAL

Try to avoid car rental. Driving in the city of Marrakech is not for the
faint-hearted and driving into the mountains is positively frightening.
can hire a car with a driver for just a little more than a car alone. If yo
determined, head to the airport or Guéliz, where all the major compan
have offices.

DRIVING

● In Morocco, drive on the right and observe the following speed lim
  as well as any signed restrictions:
  Built-up areas: 50kph (30mph)
  Highways: 100kph (60mph)
● Watch out for vehicles with no lights, mopeds and bikes at night.
● If you're travelling with children, you will need to bring your own
  child seats.

Being there

TOURIST OFFICES
Main Tourist Office
Place Abdelmoumen Ben Ali,
Guéliz ☎ 024 43 61 31

Tourist Information Office
Place Youssef Ben Tachfin,
Koutoubia
☎ 024 38 52 61

The second of these offices
(across the road behind the
mosque) is closed on Saturday
and Sundays, but the tourist police
have a booth behind and are
usually helpful.

MONEY
Moroccan dirhams (MAD or dh) can't be exchanged at home and you
can't spend them beyond passport control or even on the national
Moroccan airline, so bring your debit/credit card or travellers' cheques;
although the latter can involve poor exchange rates. ATMs are plentiful,
dotted around Jemaa El Fna and at most city banks. You may see begging
at ATMs in the medina, but bear in mind that charity is considered a duty
of Islam and begging is more acceptable here. Credit cards are widely
accepted in hotels and upmarket shops, but in the souks cash is king. For
larger purchases, the seller might accept a card.

Prices In Marrakech, hotel rates are comparable to prices at home, as is
dining out, especially if you drink wine, beer or spirits with your meal. As
for souk souvenirs, similar items are competitively priced on the internet,
but of course it all depends on how good you are at haggling.

TIPS/GRATUITIES
Yes ✓   No ✗

Hotels (if service included)	✓	10%
Restaurants (if service not included)	✓	10-15%
Cafés/bars (if service not included)	✓	10%
Taxis	✓	10%
Massage/Spa attendants	✓	5%
Doormen	✓	change
Directions	✓	change
Toilets	✓	change

POSTAL AND INTERNET SERVICES

The main PTT (post) office is in Guéliz at Place 16 Novembre, on the corner of Av. Mohammed V and Hassan II. 🕓 Mon–Sat 8am–2pm. There is also a PTT on Place Djemaa El Fna 🕓 Mon–Thu 8:30–12, 2–6:30, Fri 8.30–11:30 and 3–6:30, Sat 8:30–11:30.

More hotels and riads now have Wi-Fi facilities, and often a guests' computer for internet access. If you can't find the '@' symbol try holding down the 'Alt Gr' key to obtain it.

TELEPHONES

Most mobile phones with roaming will work in Morocco (check with your provider) but the cost is high as is dialling direct from your hotel. For short visits, buy a phonecard for public payphones from tobacconists or newspaper stands. For a long visit, bring an unlocked phone from home and buy a pre-paid Moroccan SIM at Maroc Telecom or Méditel outlets.

For all calls within Morocco use the full area code '024' (which has replaced '044') when dialling a local Marrakech number. To dial a Marrakech number from abroad, the international access code is +212, followed by the city code without the 0, then the local number.

INTERNATIONAL DIALLING CODES

From Morocco to:
UK: 00 44
Germany: 00 49
USA and Canada: 00 1
Netherlands: 00 31
Spain: 00 34

EMERGENCY TELEPHONE NUMBERS

Police: ☎ 19
Tourist Police: ☎ 024 38 46 01
Fire/Ambulance: ☎ 15

EMBASSIES AND CONSULATES

UK: ☎ 024 42 08 46
Germany: ☎ 037 65 36 05
USA: ☎ 022 26 71 51

Netherlands: ☎ 022 22 18 20
Spain: ☎ 037 68 74 70

HEALTH ADVICE

Sun advice Drink plenty of water and take regular breaks when walking. Treat dehydration symptoms (e.g. diarrhoea) as soon as possible.

Dentists, Doctors and Drugs If required, ask your hotel to recommend a reliable private dentist or médecin généraliste (GP). Bring prescriptions for any medicines you need but be aware that pharmacies may dispense drugs without controls and ask for the prescription specific brand name.

PERSONAL APPEARANCE AND BEHAVIOUR

Women who display bare arms, legs, neck or cleavage give offence but a thin shawl which covers your arms and chest will protect you, both from the sun and unwanted attention. Locals, especially women, don't appreciate being photographed as curiosities. Always ask before taking a picture – in tourist hot-spots, you might be asked for money for the privilege, which may well help feed a family.

PERSONAL SAFETY

Crime is low here, thanks to the ubiquitous plain-clothed Tourist Police, even pickpocketing is not the problem it once was.

ELECTRICITY

The local supply is 220 volts, 50Hz, using two-pin round plugs, as used in France. Remember to bring a travel adaptor from home.

OPENING HOURS

Many shops and restaurants have erratic opening time which can vary day-to-day depending on how busy they are. Shops in the New City close Sundays and the souks are closed Friday mornings but otherwise stay open until 9pm or later each day.

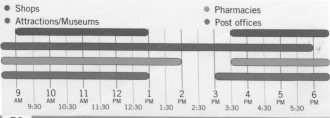

- Shops
- Attractions/Museums
- Pharmacies
- Post offices

LANGUAGE

Moroccans speak their own version of Arabic and various dialects of Berber. In Marrakech, French is widely understood and many restaurant and hotel workers understand basic English.

Do you speak English?	*Itkelim Ingleezi*	hello *(informal)*	*La bes*
I don't understand	*Mafhemsh*	response *(informal)*	*bikheer*
yes	*eeyeh, naam*	goodbye	*bislemah*
no	*la*	please	*min fadlka*
hello *(to Muslims)*	*as Salaam alaykum*		*(fadlik) /afek*
		thank you	*shukran*
Response *(to Muslims)*	*wa alaykum salaam*	God willing	*Imshallah*
I'm lost	*Ana T'left*	left/right	*yassar/yemeen*
Where is…?	*Feyn…?*	straight on	*neeshan*
mosque	*gaama; masjid*	How many kilometres?	*Kam kilomet?*
near/far?	*kareeb/baeed*		
restaurant	*mataam*	butter	*zibda*
breakfast	*iftar*	coffee	*kahwa*
lunch	*yada'a*	meat	*leham*
dinner	*chasha'a*	fish	*samak*
egg	*beyd*	chicken	*dajaj*
bread	*khobz*	I don't eat…	*Makanakulsh…*
pharmacy	*farmasyan*	pain	*alam*
clinic	*chiyadah*	diarrhoea	*is'hal*
doctor	*tabeeb*	dizziness	*dawsah*
medicine	*dawa'a*		
market	*souk*	Where is the mirror?	*Aynal mir'ah?*
It's expensive	*Innahoo galee*	enough	*kafee*
How much is it?	*Kam siaro hatha?*	open	*mahlul*
Another colour?	*Lawanan axar?*	closed	*mahdud*

Best places to see

1 City Walls and Gates

The distinctive pink ramparts encircling the medina separate the old town from the new. Today, pedestrians, scooters, cars and calèches all funnel through the decorative gates at speed.

In 1126, the Almoravid Sultan Ali Ben Youssef began constructing the 10m (33ft) high fortifications to keep out his tribal enemy, the Almohads. The city fell in 1147, but the walls remained, up to 2m (6.5ft) thick in places, with 200 towers and stretching for 6km (10 miles).

The ramparts are best appreciated in the early morning or at dusk when the sun gives them a warm, orangey glow. Blot out the traffic chaos below and look up to the high fringe of palm trees; it is almost possible to imagine life in the gardens, houses and palaces behind these walls nearly a thousand years ago.

A walk around the walls is a dusty and noisy journey. Instead, consider a calèche ride (► 29) in the evening when the traffic has died down. The full circuit takes about an hour and costs around 170Dh (€15) – but be sure to agree a price first.

These medieval walls are made of *pisé* (earth) that has proved very durable. The gates that punctuate the medina walls at irregular intervals are all individual – both in form and function. Many were added later to increase access to the medina; these newer ones are much less ornate. The most notable are decorative Bab Debbagh and Bab Agnaou (► 90), which show spectacular Moorish design.

Jardin Majorelle and Musée d'Art Islamique

www.jardinmajorelle.com

This cool blue oasis in the pink desert city is both finely designed botanic garden and relaxing retreat, with soaring palms and painterly detail.

French artist, Jacques Majorelle (1886–1962) produced restrained, obscure watercolours, while his father, Louis made furniture. Yet their most impressive work was this joint effort outside both their specialist fields. Opened in 1947, the gardens were coloured with the revolutionary, bright hue that became known as *Majorelle bleu*. When Jacques died, the garden fell into disrepair before being bought by Marrakech resident and fashion designer, Yves Saint Laurent in 1980.

A trickling fountain at the entrance gives way to a rustling bamboo forest. To the right is the garden's most memorable view through to a lily pond reminiscent of Monet. The global collection of plants includes cacti and banana trees under which visitors can sit on benches to read, to snooze or to enjoy a romantic moment. The garden is dotted with blue terracotta pots, wandering turtles and 15 species of birds, some of them rare.

Jardin Majorelle follows the design rules of all Islamic gardens, as laid out in the Koran. Enclosed by walls, with water at its

heart, it boasts lush vegetation and simple architecture. Although intended to be a serene earthly paradise, this small garden often becomes overrun with visitors. To experience the peace of the garden the best time to visit is first thing in the morning.

The old painting studio is now the intimate Museum of Islamic Art, containing Yves Saint-Laurent's personal collection, including Berber jewellery and weapons, as well as some Majorelle paintings.

✠ 5B ✉ Avenue Yacoub El Mansour, Guéliz
☎ 024 30 18 52 ⏱ Oct–May daily 8–5, Jun–Sep 8–6
✋ Expensive; separate museum entrance: moderate
🍴 Lovely courtyard cafe onsite serves delicious juices, snacks and sandwiches (➤ 59)

3 Jardin Ménara

Like a swimming lake for ancient gods, the world's grandest reservoir is the centrepiece of the Ménara garden, with its fine pavilion and spectacular mountain backdrop.

Ménara derives from *minzah*, meaning pavilion, and also 'beautiful view'. The view is best in winter and spring, when the pavilion is framed by the snow-capped Atlas Mountains (between May and September, heat haze obscures the peaks). The legend has it that sultans would entertain their lovers in this romantic setting. One particular sultan had a habit of casting guests into the waters, but today only fish disturb the peace, leaping to catch the insects.

The present pavilion was built in the 19th century, replacing one erected some three hundred years earlier. But these were just royal ornaments around a purpose-built oasis enabling crops to grow.

The lake was constructed in the 12th century, when most of North Africa was ruled from Marrakech. Underground channels, called *khettaras*, brought water from the mountains 30km (18.6 miles) away.

This is no ornamental garden and there is not a flowerbed in sight. Instead, olive groves surround and you can see olives being harvested between October and January.

There is a small charge to enter the Ménara pavilion where the upper-level view is the main attraction. Try to get there in late afternoon, when the day has cooled, the crowds have gone, and the sunset adds to the romance. The evening sound and light show is not recommended unless you like waving banners and clunky dancing.

🕀 13L 🖂 Avenue de la Ménara, Hivernage 🕾 None
🕘 Daily 8:30–6 👋 Free; pavilion entry: inexpensive (€)
🍴 Down some steps from the lake there is a pleasant café for light refreshments (€) ❓ Sound and light show

4 Koutoubia Mosque

Spiritual symbol and city landmark, this mosque is at the heart of Marrakech. Entry is forbidden to non-Muslims but the exterior more than justifies a visit.

The splendid 12th-century minaret of the Koutoubia Mosque towers above the square of Jemaa El Fna. A constant presence in Marrakech, its resounding *Adhan* (call to prayer) echoes throughout the city by day and by night it is spectacularly lit up.

At the top of the 69m-high (226ft) minaret are the loudspeakers that broadcast the *Adhan*. At most mosques, the call is pre-recorded, but here the call is recited live by the *muezzin*. From an adjacent pole, pointing to Mecca, a flag was traditionally hoist to signal the time for prayer and is still used today if the loudspeakers fail.

The *Koutoubia* (booksellers') mosque was named for the market stall holders who sold their religious manuscripts nearby as early as the 7th century. The foundations of the first building, built around 1150 by the Almohad dynasty, can still be seen through the railings next to the current mosque. Directly in front of the mosque are two glass enclosures covering the original washing areas. Here, men and women would separately wash their hands, feet and face before entering the mosque.

Surrounding the mosque are the Koutoubia Gardens which make for a pleasant stroll (► 62). Filled with roses, orange trees and bird song, ice cream vendors sell their wares to locals and tourists relaxing on benches in the shade.

✚ 1c ✉ Avenue Bab Jedid
☎ None 🍴 Koutoubia café (€)
❓ The call to prayer occurs five times a day between dawn and dusk, but not at set times. No admission to non-Muslims

5 Medersa Ben Youssef

This Koranic school is one of the few sites non-Muslims can enter. There is real serenity in the architecture – so, more than anywhere else in Marrakech, avoid it when crowded.

One of the largest centres for religious education in North Africa, Ben Youssef was founded in the 14th century. Rebuilt by the Saadians around 1570, it has not been used as a Koranic boarding school since 1960.

It can be difficult to find the school on your own, even with the aid of a map, and the entrance is through a rather dark corridor. This opens onto a beautiful, sunlit colonnaded courtyard, bathed in sunlight and dominated by a large, rectangular pool. Influenced by Andalusian architecture, around it are multi-coloured *zellij* (Moorish mosaic tiling) and intricate stucco panels. Behind it, the domed prayer hall displays intricately carved cedar wood, unusual palm motifs and inscriptions from the Koran.

Two staircases from the entrance lead up to over 100 tiny student rooms. Avoid the swarms of photographing and posing tourists who dart in and out of the honeycomb of cells. Find an empty one, shut the door and imagine the 900 students that not so very long ago shared these tiny quarters.

Information panels are only in French, but two of the rooms have been reconstructed to contain all the basic things a student would have – a mat for sleeping on, a tea set and writing desk. The *Medersa* (theological college) was used as a Sufi retreat in the film, *Hideous Kinky* (1998) starring Kate Winslet and based on the novel by Esther Freud.

✠ 3f ✉ Off souk El Khemis ☎ 024 39 09 11 ⏰ Apr–Sep
daily 9–7, Oct–Mar 9–6 ✋ Expensive; combination
ticket can be purchased to includes entrance to Musée de
Marrakesh and Almoravid Koubba 🍴 Café in Musée de
Marrakech next door (➤ 46)

6 Musée de Marrakech

www.musee.ma

The star exhibit of this museum is the building itself, with its fine central courtyard and former palace hammam now used as an exhibition space.

This late-19th century palace is an elegant expression of classical Andalusian architecture. In the centre of the cool, serene main courtyard is an impressive fountain and chandelier, surrounded by comfortable chairs – a lovely, relaxing spot. Traditional music adds to the atmosphere, CDs of which can be bought in the museum shop.

The salons and archways off the main courtyard contain interesting permanent exhibitions, where the emphasis is on traditional Islamic arts. Examples of Arabic calligraphy and some ancient Korans are here, along with Islamic coins dating back to the 8th century and traditional costumes from Fez and the Atlas Mountains.

There is also some delicate Berber embroidery, textiles and jewellery, including some notable silver hands of Fatima – a good luck charm, as well as visually powerful old black and white photos of women from the Atlas Mountains. Towards the rear, the ceramics section displaying highly

decorated pottery is not to be missed; not least for the opportunity to look up and admire the finely worked ceiling.

In the former kitchens the changing exhibitions of contemporary art are of varying quality, but some significant Moroccan artists are represented. The hammam, filled with a huge white sofa, is a delight. Even the toilet – with its traditional tiling and brass taps – is a work of art. There is limited information on the exhibitions and that is only in French.

➕ 3f ✉ Place Ben Youssef ☎ 024 44 18 93 🕐 Daily 9:30–7
✋ Expensive. Combination ticket can be purchased to include entrance to Medersa Ben Youssef and Almoravid Koubba 🍴 Pleasant courtyard café €
❓ Guided tours available. The building is air-conditioned

7 Night Market

Dine beneath a thousand stars, and beside a thousand other customers, surrounded by fortune tellers and snake charmers, in one of the largest open air restaurants in the world.

Every night at dusk, as the sun begins to set behind the Koutoubia Mosque, gas lanterns are lit and smoke from more than 100 barbecues begins to scent the air of Jemaa El Fna (► 78). This is just the beginning of the atmospheric medieval pageant, where darting boxers and dancing transvestites fill the wings.

Everyone should eat at the night market at least once. The food is fresh, usually either boiled or fried, and reports of illness are extremely rare. It's also very, very cheap, so you can experiment. This is Moroccan fast food at its best: just look and

point and a steaming and delicious meal will be on your table in minutes.

'Starvin' like Marvin?' or 'Fish and Chips?' are some of the come-ons you will hear from the multi-lingual stallholders. If it's your first time, the 'hustle' can be intimidating, but it's all in good fun, and undercover tourist police ensure restraint. 'Welcome to my air-conditioned restaurant.... Five Michelin stars' might be a joke, but these entrepreneurs offer some of the most memorable meals anywhere in Morocco.

Some stalls have menus in English and French or may specialise in just one dish, such as hard-boiled eggs or bowls of snails. Choose from juicy meat or vegetable kebabs, mixed salads, spicy sausages and perfectly cooked French fries. Tuck into a starter of bread and hot tomato dip, and don't forget to tip.

➕ 2d ✉ Jemaa El Fna ☎ No phone ⏰ Daily 6pm–midnight 👤 Inexpensive

8 Palais El Badii

No expense was spared in the building of this 'incomparable palace' (the meaning of Badii), whose ruins now house the medieval masterpiece of the *Minbar* – an exquisite 'stairway to heaven'.

Once adorned in marble, onyx and gold, this extraordinary palace was built by the Saadien king, Ahmed El Mansour. Begun in 1578, it took 25 years to build, and it took just half that time for conquering sultan, Moulay Ismail (1672–1727), to strip it bare. A hole in the three-storey-high pink dusty walls, all that is left of the gatehouse,

leads to an empty courtyard and now dry pool. This enormous complex was once filled with politicians, parties and poets, but today only birdsong and a solitary palm greet the visitor.

Only the tower on the north-eastern side retains its internal staircase; it leads to a terrace where storks and sparrows have a bird's eye view as they stand sentinel. A plan in English shows the original layout, including the Crystal Pavilion for the king, with its own pools and lounge, but only the foundations remain.

A splash of bright bourganvillea is the only indicator of the extraordinary Koutoubia Minbar (pulpit), perhaps one of the finest works of art in wood in the world. It is heavily decorated with delicate woodcarving and marquetry, with finely carved frogs and stars and verses from the Koran about Allah's dominion over heaven and earth.

The Minbar was shipped over from Córdoba, Spain where it took skilled craftsmen eight years to build. Originally used in the Koutoubia Mosque (➤ 42); a sophisticated mechanism allowed it to be wheeled out for the *imam* (priest) to use on Fridays.

🕂 4a 🖂 Place des Ferblantiers ☎ None
🕐 Daily 8:30–11:45, 2:30–5:45pm
✋ Moderate (ask for a double ticket that includes entrance to the minbar)
🍴 Kozybar (€€) 🛈 Venue for cultural events throughout the year

9 Souks

This tight, dark web of street bazaars, opening up to deep Aladdin's caves are a highlight whether you want to shop or not; just be prepared to get lost.

Stretching from the north side of Jemaa El Fna all the way up to Medersa Ben Youssef are these crowded, chaotic market stalls. They continue to be the very lifeblood of the city that began as a desert trading post. Wander down these densely packed alleyways, bustling with donkey carts and mopeds. Here, it is possible to pass 100 cupboard-sized stalls in as many metres, watched by as many pairs of eyes.

Rue Semarine forms a spine running down the middle, lined with stallholders hawking *babouches* (traditional slippers), painted tea glasses and brightly coloured leather pouffs aimed at tourists.

Traditionally each souk had its own speciality. In the northern reaches are aromatic spice stalls and carpenters' and blacksmiths' workshops. Souk des Teinturiers is the dyers' souk, full of brightly coloured wool while Criée Berbère, once the slave market, now sells carpets. The stalls around Jemaa El Fna offer over-priced, poorer quality goods.

Window-shopping is almost impossible anywhere in the souks, but watch how the locals go about their shopping and take your time, no one can force you to buy. Part of the fun is to consider what you would pay for an item, never show how much you like something and initially offer no more than a third of what you want to pay. It is a leisurely process so keep a sense of humour, accept some mint tea and if you don't quite achieve your price remember that you are dealing with some of the best salesmen in the world.

🕂 3c ✉ Central Medina ☎ No phone 🕒 Sat–Thu 9–8, Fri 12–8; with the stalls close to Jemaa El Fna (➤ 78) open until midnight 🍴 Café des Épices (Best things to do, ➤ 58) ❓ Ask a shopkeeper if you get lost (ignore young touts on the street). Since government crackdowns on pushy salesmen, who take 30 per cent commission to any purchase, guides are no longer needed

10 Tombeaux Saâdiens

Princesses and children are buried among the great rulers of the powerful Saâdien dynasty which ruled from 1524 to 1659 and was responsible for Marrakech's Golden Age.

When Moulay Ismail ordered the destruction of any example of the Saadien's success, including the Badii palace (▶ 50), he stopped short of disturbing the dead. Instead, he 're-buried' them, walling up the whole site. For several hundred years these great tombs remained untouched and they were not re-discovered again until 1917.

Ahmed El Mansour (known as Ahmed, 'the golden') ordered the construction of the tombs, along with the Badii Palace. The sultan was the first to be buried here in 1603, along with more than 60 of his entourage. Originally, the tombs were accessed through the neighbouring mosque, but a special entrance has been created for tourists. Walking through the twisting corridor, you can feel as if you are discovering them all over again.

The first room on the left is the Prayer Hall, followed by the Hall of Twelve Columns, the largest of the mausoleums, with carved cedar doors, cool Italian marble and an enormous vaulted roof. This is where Ahmed el Mansour and his family are buried. The patterned *zellij* graves for those not suitable to be buried in the mausoleum lie around a peaceful garden with wild roses, hollyhocks and apricot trees.

✚ 2a ✉ Rue de la Kasbah ☎ No phone 🕐 Daily 8:30–11:45, 2:30–5:45 ✋ Inexpensive 🍴 Sultana hotel (€€€) ❓ If you use one of the unpaid on-site guides, be sure to tip

Best things to do

Charming cafés

Café des Épices

This lovely, friendly little spot is a rare place to relax in the souks. Three floors overlook a square filled with spice and straw-hat sellers. Enjoy a mint tea, simple salads or sandwiches and take in the changing art on the blood red walls.

✉ 75 Rahba Lakdima ☎ 024 39 17 70; www.cafedesepices.net
🕐 Daily 10am–11pm

Café du Livre

Expats and jaded tourists come here for Wi-Fi, English books and magazines as well as the light, international menu created by two star Michelin chef, Richard Neat, served all day.

✉ 44 rue Tarik Ben Ziad, Guéliz (entrance via Hotel Toulousain)
☎ 024 43 21 49; www.cafedulivre.com 🕐 Mon–Sat 9:30–9pm

Café Extrablatt

A successful German franchise has brought café, bar, restaurant and disco under one roof. Take tea on the terrace of Café Extrablatt (7am–midnight); cocktails in the Artemis lounge before dinner in the Italian restaurant (6pm–1am) and move on to the disco at Be One (from 11pm).

✉ Corner of Ave. Echouada with Rue Alkadissia, next to Comptoir, Hivernage ☎ 024 43 48 43 🕙 Daily, hours vary

Grand Café de la Poste

Built in 1925 and beautifully renovated in the style of a Parisien brasserie, this café oozes old world glamour. By day, coffees and salads are served under white parasols on the breezy terrace. At night, sink into a red velvet sofa with a cocktail, soothed by live jazz and tuck into golden chicken or tender pink duck breast.

✉ Corner of Boulevard El Mansour Eddahbi and Avenue Imam Malik, Guéliz ☎ 024 43 30 38; www.grandcafedelaposte.com 🕙 Daily 8am–1am

Jardin Majorelle

Deep in the Majorelle Gardens (▶ 38) is this pretty patio café dripping with bougainvillea. Iced milk with orange blossom, old-fashioned lemonade and chilled tomato gazpacho are cooling delights, with pancakes and banana splits sweet enticements.

✉ Avenue Yacoub El Mansour, Guéliz ☎ 024 30 18 52 www.jardinmajorelle.com 🕙 Jun–Sep daily 8–6; Oct–May 8–5

Musée de Marrakech

The unassuming courtyard café sits at the entrance to the city's best museum (▶ 46). It's a good place to cool down with a fresh orange juice before braving the throngs of the medina again.

✉ Avenue Yacoub El Mansour, Guéliz ☎ 024 30 18 52; www.museedemarrakech.ma 🕙 Daily 8:30–7

Fun for little ones

All the fun of the fair at Kawkab Jeux

Fun and games can be had in this play area with fairground rides. Children can ride prettily coloured horses on the carousel, bounce on trampolines and crawl around the ball room. Pizza, ice cream, crêpes and salads can be had in the café.

✉ Kawkab Jeux , 1 Rue Imame Chafaï, Kawkab Centre Harti, Guéliz

☎ 024 43 89 29; www.kawkab-jeux.com

Join the fairy tale

Children are charmed by the magic of Jemaa El Fna (➤ 78) just as surely as the snakes in the square. At dusk, join in the dancing, drumming and handclapping of hypnotic gnawa performers (bring change for a donation). This traditional Moroccan slave music is entrancing fans of all ages worldwide.

Juicy fruit

Drink an orange juice squeezed before your eyes in the shade of the canopy of one of the brightly painted green and orange wagons in Jemaa El Fna (► 78). All the numbered stalls are good, so just pick one with your lucky number or by the size of the juice seller's smile.

Mountain adventure

Embark on a day trip to the cool Atlas Mountains (► 134), visit an ancient Kasbah and tribal Berber villages, take a picnic and enjoy riding on a donkey, or swimming in clear pools under waterfalls.

Nice ices at Ice Legend

Have a break from the snake charmers and acrobats in the main square and cool down with a choice of around 40 flavours of ice creams and sorbets to eat in or take away at this popular ice-cream parlour.

✉ Ice Legend, 52 Avenue Bab Agnaou, Place Jemaa El Fna ☎ 024 44 42 00

A splashing day out at Oasiria

At this water park you can slide down the giant toboggans, float down the 'river', and get thrown around in the enormous wave pool or by the thrilling somersault. The swimming pool and one of two children's lagoons offer calmer entertainment. There is also a volley ball court, pirate ship and restaurant.

✉ Oasiria, Km 4, Route de Barrage ☎ 024 38 04 38 ⏰ Daily 10–6
🚌 Free Shuttle service

Gorgeous gardens

Jardins de l'Agdal

In a city surrounded by desert, greenery means luxury. *Agdal* is Berber for reservoir and the Agdal Gardens are the oldest in Marrakech, created by the Almohads in the 12th century. (➤ 91)

Jardin Majorelle

The 'folly' of a French painter, these gardens became a major tourist attraction following restoration by Yves Saint Laurent. Filled with bourgainvillea, banana trees and bird song, this work of art continues to delight all its visitors. (➤ 38)

Jardin Ménara

Although one of the greenest things in the Ménara Gardens may be the roof of the pavilion, this enclave, encircled with Cypress trees, once provided privacy for a sultan to meet his mistresses. Only just out of the city, this still intimate retreat is very refreshing and feels like a world away. (➤ 40)

Koutoubia Gardens

Even in the medina, a park or garden is never far away, whether a little triangle of land to rest awhile on a bench, or the manicured gardens surrounding the Koutoubia Mosque. Minutes from the mahem of Jemaa El Fna are these well-kept gardens with blooming roses and lush green lawns watered by sprinklers. (➤ 43)

La Palmeraie

The Palmery, named after its thousands of date palm trees where grazing camels can still be seen, is now known as much for its five star hotels, luxury villas and prime real estate. (➤ 123)

Modern Marrakech

Garden of the future – Moulay Abdessalam Cyber Park

A royal park filled with ancient palm trees has been transformed into a 'cyber park', sponsored by high tech companies such as Philips and Microsoft. It is an 8-hectare Wi-Fi zone (although few laptops can be seen) dotted with rather ugly, and not always functioning, internet terminals. Ironically, most Marrakechis come here to escape the traffic-clogged streets of the 21st century city and to relax by one of the fountains or in the shade of an orange tree.

✉ Avenue Mohamed V, (entrance opposite Ensemble Artisinal) ☎ No phone; www.arsatmoulayabdeslam.ma
🕐 Daily 9am–7pm 👆 Free

Mega resort – Amanjena

The New City becomes newer every minute, with more than 100 large international resorts being built. Amanjena is an enormous resort from the Aman chain. Like modern-day sultans, celebrities and the well-heeled hole up in air-conditioned pavilions, with private pools, minibars and DVD players. This new-build palace, loosely emulating Moorish design, offers very little local flavour but is incredibly soothing and oh-so-discreet.

✉ Route De Ouarzazate, Km 12, Marrakech
☎ 024 40 33 53; www.amanjena.com

For the jet set – Nikki Beach

Nikki Beach is a stylish swimming pool/club/bar/restaurant complex which has already proved successful in Miami and St Tropez. Expensive and exclusive, day visitors pose on Balinese beds, at the swim-up cocktail bar and in the lagoon-shaped pool. This is where young, fashion-conscious Moroccans, wearing skimpy bikinis or showing off their muscles, can knock back European-priced champagne and party, hidden from the rest of Muslim Marrakech and its traditional values.

✉ Circuit de la Palmeraie ☎ 024 36 87 27; www.nikkibeach.com ⏱ Daily 10:30–2am

Super club – Pacha

The well-known Ibiza nightclub, Pacha, has been brought to Morocco, its creators boasting it is the biggest nighclub in Africa. Revellers come dressed to impress with the option to chill-out in the lounge, relax by the pool (open only in fine weather), or to eat in one of several restaurants (► 125). Mostly though, they come to dance the night away to the sounds of internationally famed DJs.

✉ Boulevard Mohamed VI ex. Avenue de France ☎ 024 38 84 00; www.pachamarrakech.com ⏱ Daily 8pm–5am

Romantic riads

La Sultana (€€€)

Live like royalty in the heart of the Kasbah in a luxurious suite with fireplace and marble bathroom, lounging in the heated pool, spa and jacuzzi. A deserved member of the 'Great Hotels of the World' group, one of the few riads in the medina with taxi access.

✉ 403 Rue de la Kasbah ☎ 024 38 80 08; www.lasultanamarrakech.com

Riad Al Massarah (€€)

The serene cream courtyard and pool is breathtakingly beautiful. Unlike some stylish riads, it has been designed with comfort (as well as the environment) in mind, with warm duvets and energy-saving real fires. Wi-Fi, hammam, massage, a superb chef and classical music fills the air. The owners invest in their staff which is not always the case.

✉ 26 Derb Djedid, Bab Doukkala ☎ 024 38 32 06; www.riadalmassarah.com

Riad Enija (€€€)

Wonderfully eclectic – many of the carved wooden doors and lamps are actually from India – and a magical place to stay. Dining in the bird-filled garden, while serenaded by musicians, is enchanting. The pool is rather tucked away and there's no hammam, but the massages are sublime. No credit cards.

✉ 9 Derb Mesfioui, Rahba Lakdima ☎ 024 44 09 26; www.riadenija.com

Riad Farnatchi (€€€)

Book suite 1 for your very own mini riad and be soothed by the sound of your private fountain. Enjoy a candle-lit supper or a barbecue for two on the roof, snuggle up on one of the *b'hous* (covered sitting areas), or get scrubbed down in the hammam. The superb, hushed service puts this riad in a league of its own.

✉ Derb el Farnatchi, Rue Souk El Fassis, Qua'at Ben Ahid
☎ 024 38 49 10/12; www.riadfarnatchi.com

Riad Tizwa (€–€€)

A simply charming and relaxed, very reasonably priced, riad. Consider booking room 2 – on its own on the roof terrace, or room 3 with its ensuite hammam. All rooms have iPod docking stations. Stay in bed all day if you like – breakfast is served until supper.

✉ 26 Derb Gueraba, Dar El Bacha. ☎ 068 19 08 72; www.riadtizwa.com

Souvenir shopping

Babouches
When picking these traditional slippers just make sure they are stitched and not glued, and real leather and not a plastic imitation. The brave can go for the yellow, pointed-toe version.

Carpets
A traditional and practical buy, which can be folded to form a compact parcel to take home.

Lanterns
Some of the most stylish hotels in the world now display the huge silver candle lanterns so common in riads.

Leather
Whether it's a fuchsia pouf or a camel skin handbag, the city is a mecca for leather.

Jellabahs
Admittedly not suitable for every social occasion, these hooded, ankle-length caftans can be bought in wool or in linen.

Jewellery
Choose from tribal Berber, antique silver and ethnic beads.

Tagine
The decorative pots are for display only; for an ovenproof tagine go for the terracotta version.

Tea glasses
Although you may never use them for tea back home they make charming candle holders. Look for hand-painted rather than machine-decorated.

Touareg spoons
With delicate, rainbow-striped handles, these are a work of art from the nomads of the Sahara.

Traditional soap
Wonderfully portable – choose from sweet-smelling rose, jasmine or almond.

Stunning views

Atlas Mountains
Snow-capped for much of the year, they form a spectacular backdrop to the pink city (➤ 134).

Essaouira
The name of this pretty seaside town means 'image' and the dramatic ramparts viewed against the blue sea and whitewashed buildings is a classic one (➤ 142).

Jardin Ménara
Ménara means 'beautiful view' and the sight of the Atlas Mountains behind the pavilion reflected in the lake is not to be missed (➤ 40).

Night market
Eager amateur photographers fight for the best vantage point over the night market on café rooftops all around Jemaa El Fna (➤ 48).

Tizi-n-Test Pass
The view from this mountain road of the valley below is awe-inspiring. At 2,100m (6,892ft), it is one of the highest in Morocco (➤ 138).

Exploring

Marrakech is a typical Moroccan city; the old town at its centre is an Arab medina with a tangle of alleyways spiralling off from a large communal square. Outside the medina is the 20th-century new town, planned in the grand European style.

From the medina's main square, Jemaa El Fna, arteries shoot north to the souks and south to the Koutoubia Mosque and the royal Kasbah. This symbolic triad is the core of Marrakech. The French built the New City with its wide, Parisian-style streets and the grand Avenue Mohamed V, which today roars with chaotic traffic.

Unlike the rest of Morocco, Marrakech, which began as a tiny caravan outpost, has huge numbers of international tourists that can overwhelm many of its architectural gems on small sites, so try to visit early in the morning.

Central Medina

The irregular shaped central 'square' of Jemaa El Fna is the beating heart of the medina and the star attraction of the whole city.

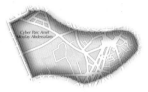

Jemaa El Fna (pronounced by quickly tripping the letters over your tongue, running one into the other) is the one open space in the often maze-like streets to its north and south. As old as the city itself, it still performs its original function as market place, theatre space and meeting point.

For the purposes of this book, the Central Medina region covers a compact area including Jemaa El Fna square and its immediate surrounds, as far as the Koutoubia Mosque. This is a section of the city densely packed with people, animals and market stalls, and where visitors will spend much of their time, day and night.

CAFÉ DE FRANCE

The slightly scruffy rattan chairs, portly waiters and ancient ceiling fans preserve this café's faintly colonial air. The throngs of Jemaa El Fna are within touching distance from the pavement terrace; the small, half-heartedly air-conditioned restaurant can be uncomfortable. Two unassuming upper terraces tend to be less crowded spots than Café Argana or Café Glacier from which to see the night market (➤ 48).

✚ 3d ✉ Place Jemaa El Fna ☎ No phone
🕔 Daily 8am–midnight

CALÈCHE RIDES

These horse-drawn carriages, for up to five people, can be a fun way for a sightseeing tour or to travel to sights such as the Majorelle Gardens (➤ 38). Increasingly heavy traffic diminishes the romantic element, unless you manage to take a trip in the evening. Although the government introduced fixed hourly prices, it is almost impossible to get drivers to keep to them. Do be prepared to bargain and always agree a price beforehand.

✚ 2c ✉ Place de la Foucauld 🕔 Daily 8am–midnight

ENSEMBLE ARTISANAL

This rather ramshackle, government-run craft complex allows visitors to see craftsmen at work, making fixed-price goods. Although not as slick or as comprehensive as its sister store, Centre Artisanal, this collection

of artisan items is more central and less claustrophobic with a pleasing courtyard and café. For larger items, you will usually pay a third more than at market stalls, but without the often tortuous bargaining process. Smaller items are often roughly the same price and generally of better quality than those in the souks – where you should watch out for plastic slippers sold as leather, for example. Dedicated shoppers come here to check prices before heading off to bargain in the souks, and it is a relaxed place to browse away from the high-pressure atmosphere of the market stalls. Watch out for disinterested shopkeepers and unscrupulous stallholders who fail to display price tags.

✚ 19H ✉ Avenue Mohamed V ☎ 024 38 68 76 ⏰ Mon–Sat 8:30–7
🍴 Courtyard café (€)

JEMAA EL FNA

Sandwiched between the Koutoubia Mosque and the souks is Jemaa El Fna, whose name means 'Assembly of the Dead'. Art, drama and religion, as well as the necessities of life, are played out here in front of the watchful eyes of tourists who fill the various viewpoints of overlooking rooftop cafés. Hypnotised, they sit and watch the captivating spectacle of fortune-tellers, garishly garbed water sellers brandishing copper cups, medicine men and tooth pullers.

Circus space, health centre and boxing ring; all teeming life is here. As well as snake charmers, acrobats and cruelly chained monkeys, you'll find storytellers – who are, quite literally, part of a dying breed. For a fee, they conjure up dramatic tales from *1001 Arabian Nights* for young audiences, while older audiences prefer religious tales. Unfortunately, television is fast replacing this skilled oral art. Henna tattooists – invariably women – are among the most insistent and sinister of sellers, hunched beneath umbrellas, their implements poised.

UNESCO recognised Jemaa El Fna as a 'Masterpiece of the Oral and Intangible Heritage of Humanity' in 2001. It soon became pedestrianised to protect its continued existence as an impromptu cultural centre, but it is still often necessary to dodge donkeys and mopeds, not to mention the occasional sleeping snake. This is authentic entertainment, not set up for the benefit of tourists and the greater part of the entranced audience is Moroccan. It is a good idea to bring some dirhams in change, as all the entertainment, including taking photographs, has to be paid for.

Nearly 50 orange juice sellers hawk their wares, calling out their cart number. Oranges are cheap and juicy and the juice is squeezed before your eyes. Pick a stallholder who is friendly, and don't let them overcharge you (prices should be clearly displayed). At dusk, a whole different story unfolds when the night market (➤ 48) kicks off and thousands of hungry visitors throng the square for the food stalls.

✚ 2d ✉ Jemaa El Fna ⑪ Café de France (➤ 76)

KOUTOUBIA MOSQUE

Best places to see, ➤ 42.

NIGHT MARKET

Best places to see, ➤ 48.

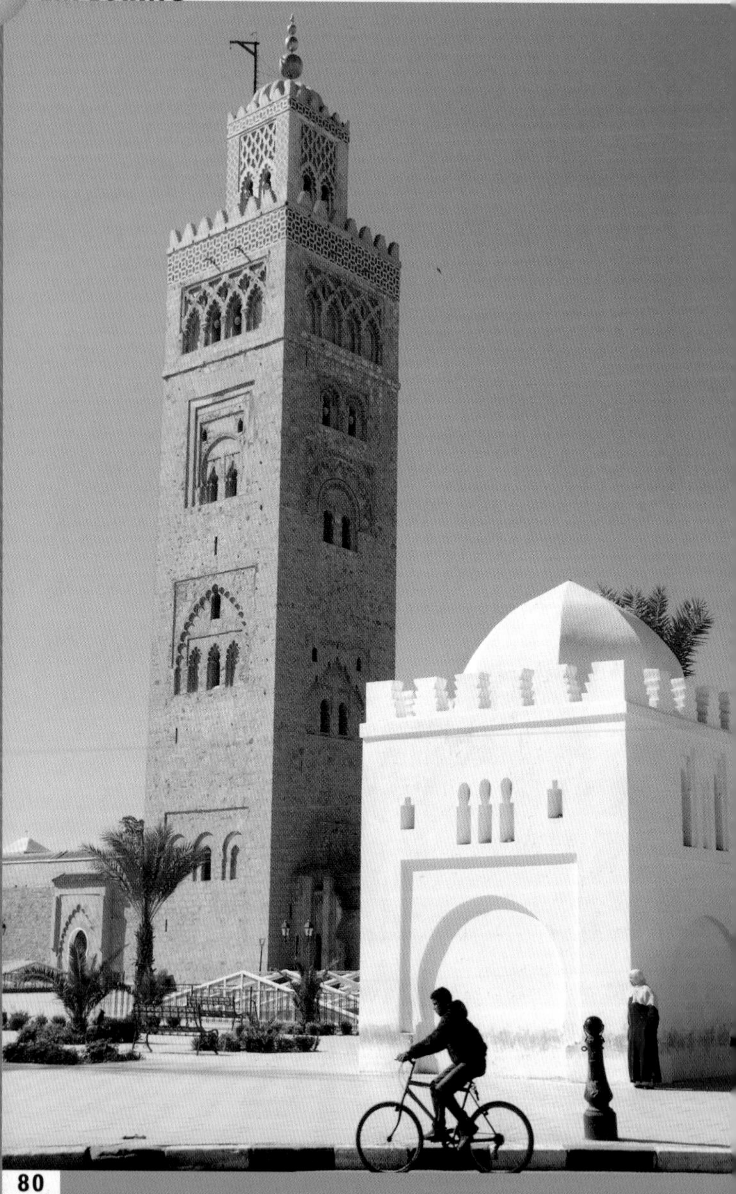

PLACE BAB FTOUH

In the small square of Bab Ftouh, tucked away between Jemaa El Fna and the souks, tea glass sellers vie for attention with miniature, air-conditioned boutiques. In a little nook on its southern edge, are dedicated olives stands, piled high in black and green edible pyramids. In the north-western corner of Bab Ftouh is Souk Fondouk Ouarzazi. Merchants once travelled across the Sahara from as far away as Timbuktu and the Sudan to trade silks, spices and even slaves in the souks of Marrakech. They slept in the upstairs galleries of the *fondouks* (former inns); the central courtyard accommodating their horses. Some fondouks are up to 500 years old and quite literally falling apart, others like Ouarzazi have been turned into a kind of Moroccan mini mall for antiques with prices to match Liberty, London's luxury department store.

✚ 2d ✉ Place Bab Ftouh ⏱ Closed Friday morning, most stalls are open by 9am and do not pack up until midnight 🍴 Café de France (➤ 76)

TOMB OF LALLA ZOHRA

Standing in the shadow of the Koutoubia Mosque (➤ 42) is the unassuming, castellated, *koubba* (domed mausoleum) of Lalla Zohra. This daughter of a 17th-century religious leader was both a real and mythical figure. Said to be a woman by day and a white dove at night, she was worshipped by women both to increase their fertility and to protect their children – who would often be dedicated to her. The windows and door of the mausoleum have long been blocked-up and it is no longer open to the public. Painted icing-white and castellated, the tomb sits humbly on the large open square in front of the soaring Koutoubia Mosque. Next to the buzzing traffic of Avenue Mohamed V, it is easily overlooked.

✚ 1c ✉ Avenue Mohamed V, in front of the Koutoubia Mosque ☎ No phone
🍴 Café Koutoubia (€)

a walk

through the heart of Marrakech

This walk takes in central Marrakech's key sights. Beginning in Jemaa El Fna (➤ 78), it circles the Koutoubia Mosque (➤ 42) and gardens, ending up on the edge of the souks (➤ 52) and Souk Fondouk Ouarzazi. Taking easy to follow routes, it is best done in the early morning when it's cooler.

Begin with a coffee at Café de France (➤ 76) or a fresh orange juice at one of the stalls on Jemaa El Fna.

Cross the square to Place de Foucauld, passing the calèches (➤ 29). Be careful when crossing busy Avenue Mohamed V to the Koutoubia Mosque, then turn left immediately in front of it to walk through the Koutoubia Gardens around the back of the mosque.

There are pretty lawns behind the mosque and a fountain (often dry) next to an English-looking bandstand on right. It's a lovely spot to pause a while.

Follow the path next to the Koutoubia back to the main road, with the Tomb of Lalla Zohra (▶ 81) on your left. Cross the zebra crossing with care, drivers don't stop at such crossings automatically, past Café Koutoubia (▶ 43). Walk over a second zebra crossing Rue Fatima Zohra and along pedestrianised Rue de la Koutoubia (no sign).

Stop at the Hotel Jardins de la Koutoubia (▶ 84) for lunch or a drink by the pool, or for a different culinary experience pop upstairs to the Asian terrace restaurant, Les Jardins de Bala (▶ 86).

Turn left out of the hotel, continuing along Rue de la Koutoubia, which kinks to the left. A little further on, to the right, are traditional basket sellers. Continue straight on, over the corner of Jemaa El Fna, to Bab Ftouh (▶ 81), before returning to Jemaa El Fna.

Distance 2km (1.2 miles)
Time 2 hours including lunch
Start/end point Place Jemaa El Fna ✚ 2d
Lunch/Dinner Hotel Les Jardins de la Koutoubia (€€–€€€)
✉ 26 rue de la Koutoubia ☎ 024 38 88 00

HOTELS

Les Jardins de la Koutoubia (€€€)

Highly recommended, and one of the few places to stay in the old town offering luxurious, yet child-friendly accommodation. Charming staff, three swimming pools, three great restaurants, and a spa (like most hotels in Marrakech) open to non-guests.

✉ 26 Rue de la Koutoubia ☎ 024 38 88 00;
www.lesjardinsdelakoutoubia.com

Jnane Mogador (€)

A simple hotel, it is one of the best budget options, with consistently good reviews. Sometimes difficult to book so make sure you get confirmation. Breakfast and dinner are extra. Hammam and rooftop with great views, and a really good location.

✉ 116 Riad Zitoune, Derb Sidi Bouloukat ☎ 024 42 63 23;
www.jnanemogador.com

L'heure d'Eté (€–€€)

This is a no-frills, reasonably priced town house, with a few rules about checking out, etc. It is clean, friendly and close to Jemaa El Fna, with breakfast served on the rooftop terrace.

✉ 96 Sidi Bouloukat ☎ 024 39 17 27; www.lheure-dete.com

Marrakech La Medina (€€€)

In a very special location; nightly drumming from Jemaa El Fna can be heard from the lovely courtyard and pool. Expect an international clientele on all-inclusive packages. Spa, sports club and excellent cuisine.

✉ Jemaa El Fna ☎ 024 44 40 16; www.clubmed.co.uk

Riad Lotus Ambre (€€–€€€)

This is a slick, stylish operation with Indian-Syrian décor. A boutique hotel, even though there are several Riad Lotuses in the city. Attention to detail sometimes slips but generally good personal service.

✉ 22 Fbal Zefriti ☎ 024 43 15 37; www.riadslotus.com

RESTAURANTS

Café de France (€–€€)
See page 76.

Café Glacier (€–€€)
The top floor terrace may be the best vantage point from which to view the night market. However, the turn-style entry, compulsory drink purchase and scrum of camera-wielding tourists are decidedly unappealing. Consider visiting during the day instead.
✉ Hotel CTM, Jemaa El Fna ☎ 024 42 23 25 ⏰ Daily 8am–midnight

Chez Chegrouni (€)
It's hard to fault this simple, long-standing place serving kebabs, chips, salad and soups. A recent face-lift means no more writing orders on a napkin before settling down at your table.
✉ Jemaa El Fna ☎ 024 65 47 46 ⏰ Daily 7am–11pm

Club Med La Medina (€€€)
It's a bit of a secret that this exclusive enclave catering to a predominantly French clientele is open to non-residents for both a themed, varied buffet and a very good lunch.
✉ Jemaa El Fna ☎ 024 44 40 16; www.clubmed.co.uk ⏰ Daily lunch 1–3, dinner buffet 8pm–9:30pm

Les Jardins de Bala (€€)
Although billed as Indian food, the dishes here, such as vegetarian stir-fries and tapas have a distinctly Asian – even European – bent. Attentive service and a rooftop with a wonderful view of the mosque are major draws.
✉ 26 Rue de la Koutoubia ☎ 024 38 88 00; www.lesjardinsdelakoutoubia.com ⏰ Daily 12–3:30, 7:30–12

Les Jardins de la Koutoubia (€€)
The French and international lunch time menu, with excellent service, is served at the open air pool-side. The dishes are light and well presented making this a much better option than the

sometimes stuffy, although very good, restaurant in the evenings.
Dishes include excellent salads and steaks, delicious ice cream
and sorbets and the service is charming and efficient.
✉ 26 Rue de la Koutoubia ☎ 024 38 88 00;
www.lesjardinsdelakoutoubia.com 🕙 Daily 12–4

Les Terasses de'Alahambra (€–€€)

One of the more comfortable and nicest places to eat on the
square, with a simple menu of salads – Nicoise and warm goat's
cheese, Morrocan dishes and good, thin-crust pizza. Cooling ice
creams and sorbets are available in children's portions.
✉ Jemaa El Fna ☎ 024 42 75 70 🕙 Daily 8am–11pm

Night Market (€)

Consistently excellent food, such as spicy sausages, fish and
chips, delicately fried squid, and vegetable kebabs, is dished up
here with bread and spicy sauce. This freshly cooked food is as
good as you will get anywhere in Morocco. See also page 48.
✉ Jemaa El Fna ☎ No phone 🕙 Daily dusk to midnight

Pizzeria Venezia (€€)

Very good pasta, pizza and salads are on offer in this first floor
pizzeria, but no alcohol due to the proximity to Koutoubia Mosque.
There are great views at sunset from the breezy terrace.
✉ 279 Avenue Mohamed V (upstairs) ☎ 024 44 00 81
🕙 Daily 12–3pm, 6:30–11:30pm

Portofino Ristorante Pizzeria (€€)

This low-lit Italian restaurant looks rather like a pizzeria chain and is
popular with westerners. Pizza, pasta and salads, as well as beef
and seafood are on the menu.
✉ 279 Avenue Mohamed V ☎ 024 39 16 65 🕙 Daily noon–11pm

Restaurant Relais de Paris (€€)

This intimate restaurant next to a large swimming pool is an
elegant spot and is renound for the quality of its service. Rib

steak with home-made chips and grilled duck breast are stand-outs from the concise menu.

✉ 26 Rue de la Koutoubia ☎ 024 38 88 00; www.lesjardinsdelakoutoubia.com 🕐 Daily 2–3:30, 7:30–12

Le Riad Des Mers (€€)

This is a friendly place where fresh fish and seafood, such as oysters and lobsters, are brought in daily from the coast and there are also some Italian favourites, offering a change from traditional tagine fare.

✉ 411 Derb Sidi Messaoud ☎ 024 37 53 04; www.ilove-marrakesh.com/riaddesmers 🕐 Daily 8pm–midnight

SHOPPING

Akbar Delights

This tiny shop sells finely embroidered slippers and textiles with an Asian influence that wouldn't be out of place on the Champs-Élysées; prices reflect this.

✉ 45 Place Bab Ftouh ☎ 071 66 13 07 🕐 Tue–Sun 9:30am–1pm, 3:30–7pm

Beldi

Upmarket boutique selling at European prices at the entrance to the medina. On sale is tailoring by two brothers in desirable fabrics with a contemporary flair.

✉ 9–11 Rue Mouassine, Bab Ftouh ☎ 024 44 10 76 🕐 Daily 9–9

Boutique Bel Hadj

Tucked up in the top of this fondouk, the owner Bari, presides over his treasure trove of jewellery – much of it tribal – from as far away as China, Nepal and the Ivory Coast. Again, no bargains.

✉ Souk Fondouk El Ouarzazi 22–23 (upstairs) ☎ 024 44 12 58 🕐 Daily 9–8

Fibule le Sud de Sahara

The smiling shop owner, selling Berber and Touareg jewellery, dresses in the traditional Touareg bright blue caftan and turban.

✉ Souk Fondouk El Ouarzazi 27 (upstairs) ☎ 070 96 52 73 🕐 Daily 9–8

ENTERTAINMENT

Café Arabe

One of the few places where you can buy alcohol in the central medina, but not the only reason to come here. Serving excellent cappuccinos and pretty pastries. It's also a sophisticated, candle-lit lounge bar/restaurant with music and Italian/Moroccan food.

✉ 184 Rue Mouassine ☎ 024 42 97 28; www.cafearabe.com

⏰ Daily 10am–midnight

Grand Tazi Hotel

This really is the only place around Jemma El Fna to get a cheap beer. The haunt of backpackers, it has a relaxed atmosphere.

✉ Corner of Ave El Mouahidine and Rue Bab Agnaou ☎ 024 44 27 87

⏰ Daily 10pm–11pm

Kssour Agafay

As parts of Marrakech become ever more exclusive, this members club will cater to a growing need. Kssour Agafay Town and Country Club is a hotel and spa outside of the city

✉ 52 Sabet Graoua ☎ 024 42 70 00; www.kssouragafay.com

⏰ Daily noon–midnight

Piano Bar Ouarzazi

The snug little corner of this luxury hotel nightly serves very decent cocktails to the tinkling from the resident pianist, creating a not particularly Moroccan, but very pleasant, atmosphere.

✉ 26 Rue de la Koutoubia ☎ 024 38 88 00;

www.lesjardinsdelakoutoubia.com ⏰ Daily 6pm–midnight

Souk Cuisine

This cookery course is a highly recommended 'taste' of Morocco that offers a real insight into local culture at very reasonable cost including lunch and wine. First to the market to buy ingredients and then to the owner's house to create traditional Moroccan dishes.

✉ Zniquat Rahba, 5 Derb Tahtah ☎ 073 80 49 55; www.soukcuisine.com

⏰ Courses daily 10–4; dinner courses on request

Southern Medina

The Kasbah, the royal quarter, is here, site of two magnificent ancient palaces and some striking royal tombs.

The Agdal Gardens are still used by the royal family and are only open sporadically. The historic Mellah, the Jewish quarter, two interesting museums and the shopping mecca of Centre Artisanal are the key points of interest. The modernist King, Mohamed VI's new palace (not open to the public) is here too – built, not without some controversy, as a smaller version of the existing palace. This is where the King and his family stay when they visit from the capital, Rabat.

This area covers the medina south of Jemaa El Fna, from where it is an easy enough walk, depending on the heat (➤ 82). If you decide to take a taxi, walk to the edge of Jemaa El Fna, as taxi drivers charge an inflated price from the square itself; a short calèche ride is another option.

BAB AGNAOU

Guarding the entrance to the Kasbah, Bab Agnaou was built in the 12th century by the Almohads. One of their masterpieces, it is the most striking gate in the city walls (➤ 37) with intricate concentric arches, floral details and inscriptions from the Koran. Constructed for decoration, rather than defence, Bab Agnaou was certainly even more imposing at one time. Rebuilt and reduced over the years, it is currently in need of restoration.

✚ 2a

CENTRE ARTISANAL

This centre is a virtual department store of Moroccan items made by artisans. The lower ground has smaller items of most interest to visitors; the upper floors are mostly furniture and carpets. The big attraction is the fixed prices, but shopping here is not without its frustrations. Not all goods are marked and it can be hard to get (and keep) the attention of sales assistants. They are not always well informed about goods, for example, insisting that an obviously viscose dress is silk. But it's a great one-stop shop and credit cards are accepted.

✚ 21L ✉ 7 Derb Baissi Kasbah, Boutouil ☎ 024 38 18 53; www.bouchaib.net 🕐 Daily 8:30–7:30

DAR SI SAID

The brother of the man who constructed the Palais de la Bahia (➤ 96) built this late 19th-century palace, which today houses the Museum of Muslim Arts. Signs guide visitors through a series of rooms displaying elegant furniture, traditional Berber jewellery and finely decorated wooden doors. The building, with its traditional three floors and central courtyard, is a museum piece in itself, with extraordinary carved ceilings and some pretty gardens.

✚ 4c ✉ Derb El Bahia, Riad Zitoun El Jedid ☎ 024 44 24 64 🕐 Wed–Mon 9–12:15, 3:15–5:30

JARDINS DE l'AGDAL

The 12th-century Agdal Gardens were built as a royal retreat and predate even the famed Alhambra Gardens in Spain. Spread over 3km (1.8 miles) with welcome shade provided by orange, apricot, pomegranate and olive trees, they form an orchard oasis in the desert. Artificial lakes and a sophisticated watering system were created from subterranean rivers harnessed from the Ourika Valley (► 136) 30km (18.6 miles) away. In the 19th century, sultans held extravagant boating parties here, until one drowned when his vessel sank in the lake.

✚ 23M ⊗ Fri and Sun 8–5:30; closed when the King is in residence ✋ Free

KASBAH MOSQUE

The green tiled roof and the red walls of the exterior are all that non-Muslims get to see of the mosque. Located within the kasbah walls, between the Agnaou gate (► 37) and the Tombeaux Saâdiens (► 54), it is also known as the El Mansour Mosque after the sultan who built it in the end of the 12th century. Since then the mosque has been rebuilt and renovated on many occasions.

➕ 2a ❓ Closed to non-muslims

MAISON TISKIWIN

This town house belongs to Bert Flint, a Dutch anthropologist who has filled it with his treasured private collection of Berber

and Saharan artefacts. The museum is a joy for two reasons: the exhibits are well documented in English and because it's so small, it tends to be free of the tour groups that swamp other sights in Marrakech. Visitors are handed a detailed, sometimes verbose, booklet in English called *A Round Trip from Marrakech to Timbuktu*, describing the displays.

✚ 4b ✉ 8 Rue de la Bahia, Riads Zitoun ☎ 024 38 91 92 🕐 Daily 9:30–12:30, 3–6

LA MAMOUNIA
This Art Deco hotel and its impressive, 300-year-old gardens have a legendary reputation in the history of Marrakech. Despite its curent refit (closed July 2006 and its reopening severely delayed at the time of writing), La Mamounia will forever be associated with Sir Winston Churchill, who came here to paint and had a suite and piano bar named after him. Writing to President Franklin D. Roosevelt, he called it "the most lovely spot in the whole world".

✚ 19K ✉ Avenue Bab Jdid ☎ 024 38 86 00; www.mamounia.com

MELLAH
Mellahs are gated Jewish neighbourhoods found throughout Morocco that were formed to protect their inhabitants from the Arabs outside. These communities quickly became overcrowded and the impoverished people within became dirty and disease ridden. Only a few hundred Jews remain here today and very few of the synagogues that were once in every street.

✚ 4a

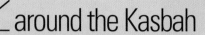

a walk around the Kasbah

This leisurely, circular route explores the royal quarter of the Kasbah, visiting two splendid palaces and two interesting museums. Try to do this walk early in the morning to avoid the heat and crowds.

Walk down Rue Riad Zitoun El Ketim, right to the end, before crossing the road to Place des Ferblantiers (▶ 96). Cross the pleasant square and turn immediately right to enter the impressive Palais El Badii (▶ 50).

Retrace your steps to the little square of the tin workers and stop for a mint tea, cocktail, or snack at Kosy Bar (▶ 103).

Leaving Place des Ferblantiers the same way you entered, turn right and immediately cross the main road, staying on the slither of uneven 'pavement' on the right-hand side.

Just before the road bends sharply to the right, you could duck into the Mellah Market (▶ 93) to cut off the corner. Otherwise, follow the bend round to the right, crossing the road to the entrance of the Palais Bahia directly on the right-hand side.

Leaving the palace, turn immediately right out of the exit (the same as the entrance) and walk along pedestrianised Rue Riad Zitoun El Jedid.

The first main alleyway on the right-hand side is reached after just a few minutes. You will see the hammam, Les Bains Ziani on the right-hand side.

Turn right immediately after the hammam, walking under an archway where you will see Maison Tiskiwin (► 92) on the right-hand side.

Take time to sit in one of the courtyards or small salons, absorbing the peaceful atmosphere of this historic house.

Leaving Maison Tiskiwin, turn right and immediately left to Dar Si Saïd (► 90) in front of you. On leaving, turn right out of the entrance and walk a very short distance to turn right onto Rue Riad Zitoun El Jedid, which leads back up to Jemaa El Fna.

Distance 2km (1.2 miles)
Time 4 hours including lunch and visits to sights
Start/end point Jemaa El Fna ✚ 2d
Lunch/Dinner Kosy Bar (€€–€€€) ✚ 4b ✉ 47 Place des Ferblantiers ☎ 024 38 03 24 ⏰ Tues–Sun noon–11pm

PALAIS DE LA BAHIA

Born a black slave, ruthless Grand Vizier (chief advisor to the sultan) Bou Ahmed built this palace at the end of the 19th century to house his four wives and two-dozen concubines. He named it Bahia ('The Brilliant') intending it to rival the finest Moorish palaces. A long courtyard entrance leads to reception halls with vaulted ceilings and female quarters opening on to banana- and palm-filled courtyards. The rooms on view are unfurnished but the architectural detail is impressive: intricately carved stucco panels, finest *zellij* (decorative tiling) and honeycombs of gilded cedar. Still used as a royal residence, most of the 150 rooms are closed to the public, although in 2001, rap singer P. Diddy filled them with super models and celebrities for a $1 million dollar party. Edith Wharton stayed in the favourite wife's room and in her book, *In Morocco* (1927) remembered the 'flowers and shadows and falling water…'.

✚ 4b ✉ Rue de la Bahia, Zitoun el–Jedid 🕐 Daily 8:30–12, 2:30–6
✋ Inexpensive

PALAIS EL BADII

Best places to see ➤ 50.

PALAIS ROYAL

The royal palace is not open to the public. What goes on behind the towering walls of this enormous complex, taking up a huge part of the Kasbah district, can only be imagined. Backing on to the mammoth Jardins de l'Agdal (➤ 91), its decorative main entrance stands in contrast with the plain pink walls. King Mohamed VI's newer, much smaller palace is on the other side of the Kasbah but some of the previous king's relatives still live here.

✚ 22L

PLACE DES FERBLANTIERS

Hidden away from the traffic is this pretty little square with benches and a simple outdoor café. It is named after the 'tinworkers' whose studios spill out over the edge of the square.

On sale are handcrafted metal lanterns, as well as ironwork lamps and mirrors – traditional and modern. Look out for the imaginative pieces made out of reworked patterned sheets of tin. Place des Ferblantiers was once called Place de Mellah, and still serves as a point of access to the Jewish quarter.

✚ 4b

TOMBEAUX SAÂDIENS

Best places to see, ➤ 54.

HOTELS

Angsana Riad Si Said (€€€)

Angsana is the sister brand of Banyan Tree Hotels & Resorts, the worldwide group famed for their impeccable service and sublime spas. Historic Si Said is just one of their six riads in the southern medina.

✉ 1–4 Derb Abbes El Fassi, Riad Zitoun Jdid ☎ 024 38 09 15; www.angsana.com

Casa Lalla (€€)

This minimalist, Moroccan-style riad offers very good value. French owned, although the Michelin chef is long gone and the breakfasts tend to be rather basic. The rooms on the ground floor get the noise of breakfast and dinner guests and are best avoided

✉ 16 Derb Jamaa, Riad Zitoun Lakdime ☎ 024 42 97 57; www.casalalla.com

Dar Les Cicognes (€€€)

Like most riads, each room is different in this luxurious boutique hotel. There's no pool, but the terraces, courtyard, library and hammam provide plenty of places for relaxation and the service rarely falters.

✉ 108 Rue Berrima, ☎ 024 38 27 40; www.lescigognes.com

Maison Mnabha (€€€)

Everything has been thought of in this 17th-century palace filled with antiques. It boasts satellite TV and five-star luxury, with real attention to detail and highly personal service. Excellent breakfasts and dinners.

✉ 32–33 Derb Mnabha, Kasbah ☎ 024 38 13 25; www.maisonmnabha.com

La Mamounia (€€€)

This historic hotel with magnificent gardens (➤ 93) was once the place to stay in Marrakech. With plenty of on-site entertainment from tennis to a casino, it is due to open in 2008 after undergoing a major, and late-running, refit.

✉ Avenue Bab Jdid ☎ 024 44 44 09; www.mamounia.com

Palais Calipau (€€€)

A relative newcomer to the exploding riad scene following a lengthy restoration, Palais Calipau offers real Moroccan hospitality in lovely and luxurious surroundings with modern amenities. Twelve suites and a pool have been lovingly created within three riads right in the centre of the medina. Breakfast is served on the roof terrace with views of the Atlas Mountains.

✉ 14 Derb Ben Zina Kasbah ☎ 024 37 55 83; www.palais-calipau.com

Riad Hyati (€€€)

Partly because it only has three rooms, but also because it is a really beautiful riad with caring staff, Hyati is often fully booked. Built in the 18th century this riad offers massages, guides and very good food.

✉ 27 Derb Bouderba, Riad Zitoun Jdid, Marrakech Médina ☎ 07770 431194 (UK); www.riadhayati.com

Riad Kniza (€€–€€€)

The owners and staff of this gorgeous riad seem to genuinely care for their guests' welfare. There are seven suites and four rooms, some have open fireplaces and all of them are spacious. One of the few Moroccan-owned riads in Marrakech. Rates includes a half-day medina tour; the mountain trips are also recommended.

✉ 34 Derb L'Hotel, Bab Doukala ☎ 024 37 69 42; www.riadkniza.com

Riad Mehdi (€€)

Great value and often fully booked, it is well worth planning ahead and booking as soon as possible. This riad is extremely comfortable: all the rooms are suites, the lounges are air-conditioned and there's a spa, garden and pool. With such attention to architectural detail, it's hard to tell it's a new build.

✉ 2 Derb Sedra, Bab Agnaou ☎ 024 38 47 13; www.riadmehdi.net

La Sultana (€€€)

See page ➤ 66.

Villa des Orangers (€€€)

This is an old Marrakech favourite. Just six rooms but, like most riads, there's a huge difference in price, size and décor. This is a rare Moroccan Relais and Châteaux restaurant serving excellent food and it also has a pool.

✉ 6 Rue Sidi Mimoun, Place Ben Tachfine ☎ 024 38 46 38; www.villadesorangers.com

RESTAURANTS

Ksar El Hamra (€€)

Musicians and oriental dancers entertain diners in this tourist-oriented restaurant serving traditional Moroccan food. Once a riad, there is formal dining in the courtyard or one of the grand salons.

✉ 28 Sabt Ben Daoud, Riad Zitoun Kedim ☎ 024 42 76 07; www.restaurant-ksarelhamra.com 🕐 Open most nights 8pm–late

Nid Cigogne (€–€€)

The snacks, salads and tagines may be mediocre, but this reasonably priced, three-storey restaurant has a rooftop terrace right ovelooking the Saadien Tombs in the Kasbah district.

✉ 60 Place des Tombeaux Saadiens ☎ 024 38 20 92 🕐 Daily 12–3pm

Palais Calipau (€€€)

Five-star food from this riad of the same rating. A simple menu (three choices of each) of Moroccan and French cuisine is available to visiting diners who book in advance. This is home-cooked cuisine in an intimate setting with highly personalised service.

✉ 14 Derb Ben Zina Kasbah ☎ 024 37 55 83; www.palais-calipau.com 🕐 Daily 7–11pm

Palais Gharnata (€€€)

Located in the Jewish quarter, where restaurants are thin on the ground, an 'evening at the palace' is as much about the surroundings, musicians and dancers as the Moroccan dishes.

✉ 5/6 Derb El Arsa ☎ 024 44 06 15; www.gharnata.com 🕐 Daily 6:30pm–12:30am

Le Sabal (€€)

The décor and atmosphere of this 100-year-old villa is self-consciously opulent. French and Moroccan food is accompanied by oriental dancers who perform in the large garden when it's warm, or inside by the fire on colder nights. Traditionally the haunt of intellectuals and artists, it is now more 'old school' than bohemian.

✉ Avenue Mohammed V and Place de la Libérté ☎ 024 42 24 22; www.lesabal.com ⏰ Daily 7pm–1am

La Sultana (€€–€€€)

Light meals and Mediterranean- and Asian-inspired cuisine can be enjoyed by the elegant pool or on the terrace. Dinner means richer French fare in the more formal restaurant. Unlike many Marrakechi restaurants, vegetarian dishes, though not always imaginative, are included on the menu. The interior is exquisite, the service in this luxury hotel is generally excellent and reservations are essential.

✉ 403 Rue de la Kasbah ☎ 024 38 80 08; www.lasultanamarrakech.com ⏰ Daily 7:30–9:30pm

Le Tanjia (€€)

One of a welcome new breed of Marrakechi restaurants that fuse traditional Moroccan food and style with a more contemporary approach. Rocket salads is on offer alongside traditional tagines. Assured, relaxed service and a pleasant rooftop.

✉ 14 Derb J'did, Hay Essalam ☎ 024 38 38 36 ⏰ Daily 10am–1am

Tatchibana (€€)

Very good, authentic Japanese sashimi, melt in the mouth tempura and barbecued meats, washed down with green tea and international wines. The simple, Zen-like space looking onto a small walled garden is a breath of fresh air.

✉ 38 Derb Bab Ksiba, Kasbah ☎ 024 38 71 71; www.tatchibana.com ⏰ Tues–Sun lunch and dinner

SHOPPING

Ayas

The exquisite silk and cotton clothing for adults and children, along with jewellery, accessories and soft furnishings here have been featured in the pages of style magazines. The shop is next door to the excellent Tanjia restaurant (► 101), so you could conveniently pick up some Moroccan designer items after lunch there.

✉ 11 Bis, Derb Jdid, Bab Mellah ☎ 024 38 34 28; www.ayasmarrakech.com
🕐 Daily 9am–9pm

Centre Artisanal

Hidden away in a corner is the oils section of this artisan centre (► 90). Pretty bottles of soothing, sweet smelling orange and rose extract are on sale that can be used to perfume the traditional argan oil that is also sold here. Made from the nuts of the rare argan tree (protected by UNESCO), this oil has been credited with dramatic moisturising properties.

✉ 7 Derb Baissi Kasbah, Boutouil ☎ 024 38 18 53; www.bouchaib.net
🕐 Daily 8:30am–7:30pm

Grand Bijouterie

The old Jewish jewellery market is a series of arcades with tiny shops shining with gold, silver and coloured gemstones. Pieces are sold by weight so know your price if you want to buy. Most of the traditional Jewish traders have long gone but it is still an interesting place to see.

✉ Rue Bab Mellah, (close to the Bahia Palace) ☎ No phone
🕐 Daily 9am–8pm

Mellah Market

This fresh food and spice market has been feeding the local population for around 500 years. Cookery classes in the city often include a visit here to purchase produce for the kitchen. The spices are fresh and exotic and if you have an interest in Moroccan food this is the place to stock up on those necessary spices. Even if you don't want to buy anything, come for the colour and atmosphere, and to photograph the enormous coloured cones of spices.

✉ Between Place des Ferblantiers and Palais Badii ☎ No phone
🕐 Daily 9am-7pm; closed Fri 9am-1pm

Mohamed Bounmentel

Attractive patterned lanterns and containers made out of tin are on sale at this little stall on the square at a fraction of the price in shops in the new town. Check for scratches and general quality before you buy.

✉ 12 Place des Ferblantiers ☎ 062 08 60 10 🕐 Daily 9am–9pm

Original Design

Ceramic tableware, as well as vases and ashtrays in an array of bright colours are on sale here. An assistant can post items around the world if you can't manage purchases in your hand luggage.

✉ 47 Place des Ferblantiers, Bab El Mellah ☎ 024 38 03 61; www.original-design-mrk.com 🕐 Daily 9am–9pm

ENTERTAINMENT

BARS AND NIGHTLIFE
Kosy Bar

A funky spot that is worth a visit any time of day, whether you drink tea from the breezy rooftop terrace, sink into deep sofas for sushi or tapas-style Thai dishes on the middle floor, or listen to evening jazz in the ground-floor piano bar.

✉ 47 Place des Ferblantiers ☎ 024 38 03 24 🕐 Tues–Sun noon–11pm

La Mamounia

Despite the rennovations that were ongoing at the time of writing, this grand old hotel is the closest thing the southern medina has to an entertainment centre and it's biggest draw is the casino (see overleaf and also page 93 for more information and contact details). Enjoy a cocktail or two in the Churchill piano bar, admire the wonderful gardens and generally soak up a little bit of the decadence this historic establishment has to offer.

Grand Casino La Mamounia

Plenty of celebrities have rolled the dice at the large which is attached to the famous hotel. Roulette, blackjack and gaming machines are some of the options for gamblers. No jeans, trainers or cameras. Passports required for pay-outs. Admittance for over 16s; gambling only for over 18s.

✉ 292 Bad Jdid ☎ Hotel: 024 38 86 00; www.mamounia.com; casino: 024 44 45 70; www.grandcasinomamounia.com 🕐 Casino: daily 3pm–5am

SPAS

Les Bains de Marrakech

Squeezed into the Kasbah quarter, this riad spa is fit for a king. If you choose the *gommage* (scrubbing), almost every crevice will be given attention, if the pressure is too much, just say: *'doucement'* (softly). Follow it with a sublime massage before chilling out in the courtyard. Bookings and payment should be made in advance.

✉ 2 Derb Sedra, Bab Agnaou, Kasbah ☎ 024 38 14 28; www.lesbainsdemarrakech.com 🕐 Daily 9am–8pm

Les Bains Ziani

Close to the Palais Bahia, this unassuming bathhouse is a good, mid-range option between the expensive, slick spas and the often basic, local hammams (where men wear trunks, and women go naked). Jacuzzi, seaweed therapy and massages are all on offer and the service is friendly.

✉ 14 Rue Riad Zitoune Jdid ☎ 062 71 55 71; www.hammamziani.ma 🕐 Daily 7am–10pm

La Sultana

Perfect for couples who can be scrubbed down together in a traditional hammam, in large hotels many spas are segregated. There are a range of packages that could keep you busy for a week. The spa of this smart hotel also has a beauty centre and hairdressers. Bookings are essential as space here is very limited.

✉ 403 Rue de la Kasbah ☎ 024 38 80 08; www.lasultanamarrakech.com 🕐 Daily 8am–8pm

Northern Medina

This large part of the medina stretches north of Jemaa El Fna to include the dense maze of alleyways known as derbs right up to the northern perimeter of the medina walls.

Immediately north of the main square is the close tangle of the souks (► 52). North again is the highest concentration of riads, in a quarter known as Mouassine. A short walk away is an important cluster of historic sights: the Musée de Marrakech (► 46), Medersa Ben Youssef (► 44) and to a somewhat lesser degree, Almoravid Koubba (► 106). To the east, the more marginal, although sociologically fascinating, tanneries are on the periphery of the medina – physically and socially. This whole quarter is dotted with mosques, historic fountains and burgeoning cultural centres.

ALMORAVID KOUBBA

At first glance, you might think this unprepossessing building has been over-run by wild roses and wilder cats, but it is worth a look for two reasons: entrance is included in the reduced 'three for one' ticket that includes the Musée de Marrakech and Medersa Ben Youssef; and less prosaically, it is the only remaining example of architecture from the Almoravid dynasty, the founders of the city.

Built by Ali ibn Yusuf in 1117, it has stood for close to a millennium but was only uncovered in the 1950s. Watch your step walking down the uneven steps to the original street level where there are some explanation panels in French only. The Koubba (dome) housed an ablutions complex, complete with showers and toilets for a long-gone mosque, and provided city residents and their livestock with water. The centrepiece is the straw, lime and stone dome with its extravagantly decorated ceiling including palm leaf and octagon motifs, and fine arches.

✚ 3f ✉ Place de la Kissaria ☎ No phone ⏰ Daily 9–1, 2:30–6 ✋ Inexpensive

BAB DOUKKALA MOSQUE

The soaring minaret of this mosque makes it a local landmark, although as with all mosques in Marrakech, non-Muslims are not allowed to enter. Built in the 16th century, with the Sidi El Hassan fountain outside, it continues to serve the thriving quarter of Bab Doukkala. From the former palace of Dar El Bacha (closed to visitors), Rue Bab Doukkala was the old road to the Berber region of Doukkala, through the gate of the same name. The ornate gate still stands, but traffic now passes through an adjacent modern gate.

✚ 7D ✉ Rue Bab Doukkala ☎ No phone ❓ Closed to non-muslims

BEL ABBES SIDI ZAOUIA

Non-Muslims can catch a glimpse of the large, open courtyard and some of the buildings of this religious complex, but are not allowed to enter. Bel Abbés Sidi was the most celebrated of seven 12th-century saints whose tombs have formed part of a popular pilgrimage since the 17th century. Bel Abbés was said to give sight to the blind, and even today the blind and handicapped are looked after here. His tomb is in a nearby cemetery.

✚ 8B ❓ Closed to non-muslims

CHROB OU CHOUF FOUNTAIN

The name of this ornate public fountain translates as 'Drink and Admire', after one of its inviting Arabic inscriptions. It was built on the orders of Sultan Ahmad al-Mansour (1578-1603), the most powerful of all Saadien rulers. Providing water for his people had spiritual as well as practical meaning, because of the Koranic importance of cleanliness. Importantly, it also showed him to be a man of charity, taste and learning. The fountain is set within a tall

recess, below a wooden arch covered in beautiful engravings and carvings.

🕂 3f ⊠ Just off Rue Bab Taghzout ☎ No phone 🖐 Free

CITY WALLS AND GATES

Best places to see, ➤ 36.

DAR BELLARJ

The 'Stork's Head' cultural centre is just north of Medersa Ben Youssef, before the mosque of the same name. The building used to be a hospital for storks, which are held sacred in Marrakech. The centre opened in 1999, with the courtyard and centrepiece fountain painstakingly restored. However, it is only really worth a special visit and the entrance fee if there happens to be an event or exhibition. Check for details in the local press and look for theatrical performances and workshops too.

🕂 3f ⊠ 9 Rue Toulat Zaouiat Lahdar ☎ 024 44 45 55 ⏰ Mon–Sat 9:30–6 🖐 Moderate

DAR CHERIFA

Hidden deep in the souks, this literary café in a beautifully restored townhouse puts on temporary, low-key art exhibitions. Lovely carved wood and stucco work frame a simple space which displays work by Moroccan and international artists. There are also casual musical performances and occasional cultural events. It's a relaxing spot for a juice or even lunch in the courtyard, and you can leaf through the books on Moroccan art and culture in the tiny library.

✚ 2e ✉ 8 Derb Charfa Lakbir Mouassine, off Rue Mouassine
☎ 024 42 64 63; www.marrakech-riads.net ⏲ Daily 10–7

MEDERSA BEN YOUSSEF

Best places to see, ➤ 44.

MINISTERIO DEL GUSTO

'The Ministry of Taste' is an eclectic, unashamedly post-Modern gallery that embraces a wide range of contemporary design. When you visit (appointments preferred) it might be showing one-off furniture pieces, or a collection of vintage fashion. Commissions for furniture design are taken here, and a wide variety of desirable *objets d'art* for the home are on sale.

✚ 2e ✉ Derb Azouz 22, el Mouassine ☎ 024 42 64 55; www.ministeriodelgusto.com ◉ Mon–Sat 9am–noon, 4–7pm

MOULAY ABDESLAM CYBER PARK

Best things to do, ➤ 64.

MUSÉE DE MARRAKECH

Best place to see, ➤ 46.

SOUKS

Best place to see, ➤ 52.

TANNERIES

The city's tanneries are perched right on the edge of the medina, not to contain the terrible stench, but for easy access to water from the Oued Issil stream which runs beyond the decorated Bab Debbagh, or tanners' gate. In a 20-day process virtually unchanged since medieval times, cow, goat, sheep and camel skins are stripped of any remaining fur and flesh (the squeamish should steer clear). The skins are then dunked into animal urine and pigeon droppings to soften them. Tanners can be seen waist deep in vats of natural dyes, such as saffron for yellow, indigo for blue and poppies for red, working in hellish conditions. Finally, the skins are dried in the sun before being made into handbags, lamps and *babouches* (Moroccan slippers). This is the sight where you will be bothered most by would-be 'guides', partly because the tanneries are quite difficult to find, but also because they want a fee for handing out mint (against the foul smell) and to show you around.

✚ 11D ✉ Rue Bab Debbagh, Tanners District ⏰ You'll find the tanners at work most days between 9:30 and 6 although it's best to visit in the morning ✋ Inexpensive

HOTELS

For additonal hotels see the selection of Romantic Riads on pages 66–67.

Dar Charkia (€€–€€€)
Nothing is too much trouble for the owners and staff of this riad, which offers a real home-from-home and a very comfortable stay. Heated swimming pool, pretty roof terrace and very good food.
✉ 49–50 Derb Halfaoui, Bab Doukkala ☎ 024 37 64 77; www.darcharkia.com

Noir D'Avoire (€€€)
This stylish English/French creation boasts sublime communal areas including a bar, lounge and rooftop. Rooms are named after African animals and three of the suites have their own jacuzzi and rooftop dining pavilion. The gym will appeal to the fit; the not-so-healthy will welcome the smoking room.
✉ 31 Derb Jdid, Bab Doukkala ☎ 024 38 09 75; www.noir-d-ivoire.com

Riad Ariha (€)
A highly recommended, excellent-value choice in this price bracket. The interior blends minimalism with traditional Moroccan design and is very light and spacious. There are five rooms in total, two of which are on the ground floor where you will find a dipping pool and a traditional hammam. There is also a Berber tent on the roof terrace. Modern touches include free Wi-Fi and satellite TV. Most of all, the staff are incredibly friendly.
✉ Sidi bin Slimane, Kaa Sour, 90 Derb Ahmed el Borj ☎ 024 37 58 50; www.riadariha.com

Riad El Fenn (€€–€€€)
Undoubtedly one of the best riads in Marrakech and justifiably one of the most expensive in this price bracket. Romantic and relaxing, with spa, pools and even a cinema. The lunch menu is light and quite simple with more formal choices for dinner. The vegetarian options are of excellent quality and all meals are made entirely

from local ingredients. The staff manage to anticipate your every need without ever intruding.

✉ Derb Moullay Abdullah Ben Hezzian, Bab El Ksour

☎ 024 44 12 10; www.riadelfenn.com

Riad Kalila (€)

Another really good value riad, where all rooms are suites. This is a typical, intimate riad with simple décor and a few nice modern touches, such as internet access and cable television.

✉ 65–66 Derb Snane ☎ 024 39 16 82; www.riadkalila.com

Riad Noga (€€–€€€)

As homely as an English bed and breakfast, complete with cascading bougainvillea.The pool, roof terrace and baths are a real draw. Appeals to older visitors and families. Closed August.

✉ 78 Derb Jdid Douar Graoua ☎ 024 37 76 70; www.riadnoga.com

Riad 72 (€€–€€€)

Delightful, Italian-run riad, with charming service. Just four rooms, including a bridal suite. Relax in the hammam, under the banana trees and enjoy the wonderful food. Special deals for families.

✉ 72 Arset Awsel, Bab Doukkala ☎ 024 38 76 29; www.riad72.com

RESTAURANTS

Café Bourganvillea (€–€€)

A riad–restaurant offering really good international and Moroccan food as well as tea and petits fours. Sit in the courtyard, shady terrace or one of the comfortable lounges.

✉ 33 Rue Mouassine ☎ 024 44 11 11 🕔 Tue–Sun 10–9

Dar Marjana (€€€)

An upmarket option, following the formula of set Moroccan menu, formal service and traditional performances. Be sure to eat either on the first floor gallery or in the garden courtyard.

✉ 15 Derb Sidi Ali Tair, Bab Doukkala ☎ 024 44 57 73;
www.darmarjanamarrakech.com 🕔 Dinner only from 8:30 pm; closed Tue

Dar Moha (€€€)

One of the best restaurants in Marrakech, although occasionally let down by a poor dish. Moroccan nouvelle cuisine served in an exquisite hundred-year-old riad. The restaurant is set around a beautifully tiled pool and its better to get a pool-side table; elsewhere can lack atmosphere. Reservations essential.

✉ 81 Rue Dar El Bacha ☎ 024 38 64 00; www.darmoha.ma
🕐 Tue–Sun 12–3:30, 7pm–midnight

Le Fondouk (€€€)

An old favourite serving consistently good food, although in a rather gloomy setting. Come for a light lunch of salmon quiche and pistachio sorbet. Evening options are richer – French dishes, such as fondant of foie gras, as well as traditional Moroccan fare and even Thai chicken.

✉ 55 Souk Hal Fassi, Kat Bennahïd ☎ 024 37 81 90;
www.foundouk.com 🕐 Tue–Sun 12–12

La Maison Arabe (€€)

This riad restaurant opened in the 1940s and is one of the city's oldest. Still retaining its colonial air, the two international and Moroccan restaurants can feel rather stuffy despite the accompanying musicians. Visit instead for cocktails and Asian-inspired tapas in the salon or tea in the courtyard garden.

✉ 1 Derb Assehbe ☎ 024 38 70 10; www.lamaisonarabe.com
🕐 Daily 8am–midnight

Le Pavilion (€€€)

Excellent French food is served in this intimate, yet formal restaurant either in cosy alcoves or in the courtyard under an enormous tree. It can be particularly difficult to find.

✉ 47 Derb Zaouia, Bab Doukkal ☎ 024 38 70 40 🕐 Daily 7pm–midnight

Le Tobsil (€€€)

Probably the best restaurant in the city. Aperitifs and drinks are included in the price of the set meal accompanied by musicians.

Tables in both the courtyard and gallery can be a little too close together for comfort but very popular nevertheless. Reservations essential.

✉ 22 Derb Abdellah Ben Hessaien, R'mila Bab Ksour ☎ 024 44 15 23
🕓 Wed–Mon 8pm–11:30pm

Terrasse des Épices (€–€€)
Sister restaurant of the Café des Épices offering salads, brochettes and chocolate desserts, as well as cultural and art evenings. Simple, yet elegant décor; chocolate-coloured rooms and a rooftop terrace with wonderful views of the medina and mountains.

✉ 15 Souk Cherifia, Sidi Abdelaziz ☎ 024 37 59 04;
www.terrassedesepices.com 🕓 Daily 9am–11pm

Yacout (€€€)
A local institution and very firmly on the map of Marrakechi restaurants, although not quite the star of the scene it used to be. Begin with an aperitif on the terrace before tucking into a three-course Moroccan feast. Reservations essential.

✉ 79 Derb Sidi Ahmed Soussi, Bab Doukkala ☎ 024 38 29 00
🕓 Tue–Sun 7pm–late

SHOPPING

Khalid Art Gallery
An eclectic collection of art and antiques from around Morocco draws international visitors and celebrities, photos of whom are pasted on the walls. Come to browse if not to buy, prices are high.

✉ Rue Dar El Basha ☎ 024 44 24 10

Kifkif
Moroccan items with a funky twist, using bright colours, pretty fabrics, delicate tailoring and fine embroidery; also more traditional raffia shoes and leather bags. Pieces are made with international tourists in mind and prices are in euros.

✉ 1 Rue des Ksours, Bab Laksour ☎ 061 08 20 41; www.kifkifbystef.com

Mustapha Blaoui

Unprepossessing and tiny from the outside, this little shop really is a cavern stacked high with affordable ceramics, lanterns and poufs, as well as high priced furniture and antiques.

✉ 142–144 Bab Doukkala ☎ 024 38 52 40

La Porte d'Or

Prices in the 'Golden Door' aren't cheap but it is a fascinating place to browse; there are hand-carved doors for sale along with finely worked, colourful Berber rugs and individual antique finds.

✉ 115 Souk Semmarine ☎ 024 44 54 54

La Qoubba

Moroccan and international art is shown at this long-standing art gallery near the Marrakech Museum, with changing and permanent exhibitions.

✉ 91 Souk Talaa ☎ 024 38 05 15; www.art-gallery-marrakech.com

ENTERTAINMENT

La Maison Arabe

Cooking workshops take place in the lovely gardens of this villa – a 20-minute taxi journey from the medina. Like most cookery courses, the emphasis is on enjoyment and participants get to eat their creations for lunch. Small groups and plenty of inspiration, as well as advice about where to buy spices and tagines in the town. See also page 114.

✉ 1 Derb Assehbe ☎ 024 38 70 10; www.lamaisonarabe.com

Riad Enija

One-day cooking courses tailored to individual needs – whether you want to know how to make your couscous fluffy, or the best way to choose spices. After a visit to the local spice market enjoy a private cooking lesson in the riad kitchen. The Riad Enija cookbook is a beautifully photographed delight, with inspiring menus to try at home. For more information see page 66.

✉ 9 Derb Mesfioui, Rahba Lakdima ☎ 024 44 09 26; www.riadenija.com

The New City

European-style entertainment and relaxation with a Moroccan twist are just a stone's throw from the medieval medina. Marrakech's two most notable gardens are here, along with a lovely little collection of chic boutiques and restaurants that wouldn't be out of place in Paris or Rome.

The French built the *Ville Nouvelle* (New Town) with its wide, leafy Parisian-style avenues between 1912 and 1956. Strictly speaking, it encompasses Guéliz and Hivernage, but today the new city is

undergoing another renewal in La Palmeraie. Here, international entrepreneurs are clearing scrubland to make way for casinos, resorts and theme parks, part of the young King's plans to bring Morocco into the 21st century. He hopes this will bring employment and improved living conditions to his people, many of whom are illiterate and living well below the poverty line. This area more than any other is Marrakech at its most modern (➤ 64).

AVENUE MOHAMED V

Mohamed V, grandfather of the current ruler, negotiated independence from France in 1956. A national hero in Morocco, the main thoroughfare in most Moroccan cities is named after him. In Marrakech, it is punctuated by the two huge roundabouts of Place de la Liberté and Place du 16 Novembre, where it intersects with Avenue Hassan II, named after the Mohamed VI's father. Parallel to the west is Avenue Mohamed VI, symbolically renamed from Avenue de France.

 4D

ÉGLISE DES SAINTS-MARTYRS

The Catholic Church of the Holy Martyrs lies just off Avenue Mohamed V. One of the first buildings in the new city, it still

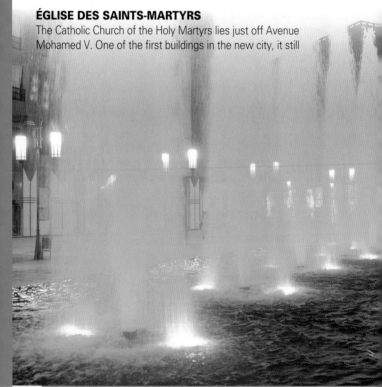

continues to serve a small church-going population. Its rather plain exterior and simple tower pales into comparison with the splendid, towering minarets of mosques in this largely Muslim city. It is thought that the name Guéliz comes from a corruption of the french word 'église'.

🚩 4E 📧 Rue El Imam Ali, Guéliz ☎ 024 43 05 85 🕐 Services Sun 12pm

GUÉLIZ

The highlights of this neighbourhood are clustered together and best explored on foot (➤ 120), visiting lovely little shops and grazing at atmospheric cafés and restaurants. Here, you will see the boldest examples of old Marrakech reinvented; where young designers sell jazzed-up camouflage *jellabahs* (traditional kaftans) and exquisite, contemporary takes on artisan jewellery. Leather from the tanneries is crafted into fashionable bags and the city's traditional lanterns have been updated for the 21st century. Guéliz has very few sights as such, but its light, bright European style shops and eateries are the perfect antidote to the exotic medieval medina. The Cimetiere Européen (European Cemetery) on Rue Erraouda provides a more sombre note. This walled burial ground dotted with mausoleums contains a white obelisk dedicated to soldiers killed in World War II and is a peaceful, well-kept spot.

🚩 4C

a walk around the Streets of Guéliz

This little circuit is something of a shopping spree, punctuated by some of the city's most charming cafes (➤ 58). Most of the boutiques here are closed for lunch from around 1pm until 3:30pm, as well as on Sundays.

Begin at Grand Café de la Poste (➤ 59) on Place du 16 Novembre.

Built in the 1920s as both a café and post office, the charming outdoor terrace is a good place to start with a bolstering coffee or snack.

Walk up Avenue Mohammed V, past the new multi-million dollar shopping mall on the right. Watch out for

the traffic as you cross Mohammed V. Turn right onto Rue Imam Malek and first left onto Rue Tarrik Ibn Ziyad. On the right hand side is Café du Livre (➤ 58,), fast becoming a local institution. Turn left onto Rue de la Liberté.

Take your time window shopping or wandering around the boutiques on this street. Many of them are air-conditioned places with young, helpful multi-lingual staff.

Cross over Ave Mohamed V, where Place Vendome (➤ 127) is on the corner and continue down Rue de la Liberté to shop at Côté Sud (➤ 127).

If you need to restore your energy and consider your what you've bought, take a break opposite at one of the most delightful eateries in this area, Kechmara (➤ 126), a great place at any time of the day.

Turn left down Boulevard el Mansour Eddahbi, a pleasant tree-lined street where you may be tempted by local offerings in the many art galleries and pavement cafes. Return to Place du 16 Novembre.

Consider a cocktail or dinner back at Grand Café de la Poste, or walk around the corner to its fine sister restaurant, Lolo Quoi (➤ 126).

Distance 1.5 km (1 mile)
Time 2 hours including lunch
Start/end point Place du 16 Novembre ✚ 4D
Lunch/Dinner Kechmara (€-€€) ✉ 3 Rue de la Liberté, Guéliz
☎ 024 42 25 32; www.kechmara.com ◷ Mon–Sat 7am–midnight

HIVERNAGE

This exclusive residential area west of the medina is known mostly for its sprawling villas and five-star, international chain hotels. While this was once the area for upmarket hotels and entertainment, the focus has very definitely moved to La Palmeraie, and the Hivernage now seems rather staid in comparison. Most visitors will come at night to eat and be entertained at Le Comptoir (➤ 126), perhaps passing the defunct Palais des Congrès on the way to the Ménara Gardens (➤ 40).

JARDIN MAJORELLE AND MUSÉE D'ART ISLAMIQUE

Best place to see, ➤ 38.

JARDIN MÉNARA

Best place to see, ➤ 40.

MARCHÉ CENTRAL

The covered Central Market on Avenue Mohamed V, north-west of Place du 16 November, was constructed in the 1920s and was the corner stone of local life but in 2005 it was razed to the ground

to make way for the Eden development, a multi-million dollar shopping mall, with luxury apartments and underground parking.
✚ 4D

THÉÂTRE ROYAL

Respected Moroccan architect, Charles Boccara designed this Royal Theatre, with its splendid portico and dome. Inaugurated in 2001, the theatre is a key venue for the annual Popular Arts Festival in July, when there are nightly musical and theatrical performances. It also hosts the Moroccan Philharmonic Orchestra several times a year. The pièce de résistance is the 1200-seat open-air amphitheatre, adding extra drama to opera and dance performances. Shows and exhibitions are held throughout the year, and a full calendar of events is available from the tourist office.
✚ 2E ✉ 40 Avenue Mohamed VI, Guéliz ☎ 024 43 15 16

LA PALMERAIE

Named after its 12th-century date palm plantation, La Palmerie flourished in the desert thanks to a sophisticated irrigation system. Nowadays, it is a patchwork of luxury rural resorts and dusty building sites – definitely not an area for sightseeing. Dubbed the Beverley Hills of Morocco, there are multiplying golf courses, extravagant restaurants and European-style nightclubs.
✚ 10A

HOTELS

Amanjena (€€€)
See page 64.

Caravanserai (€€)
On the fringes of La Palmeraie, an effortlessly stylish, rustic resort, with rooms around a patio garden. Relax in the heated pool (open to day guests), or go camel trekking or quad biking in the nearby countryside.
✉ 264, Ouled Ben Rahmoune ☎ 024 30 03 02; www.caravanserai.com

Casa Taos (€€)
Rather a grand house with gardens and a large swimming pool. The rooms inspired by famous artists and the pink and blue Frida Kahlo suite is undeniably the prettiest. Like most hotels out of the medina, it is a place to relax and unwind, then perhaps combine your stay with a few days in the city itself.
✉ Km 8, Route de Souilha ☎ 061 20 04 14; www.casataos.net

Es Saadi Gardens and Resort (€€–€€€)
Extraordinarily luxurious resort hotel in enormous grounds dating from the 1960s heydays. There are 150 rooms and 15 luxury apartments, and over 100 suites and 10 individually decorated villas, each with its own pool and garden.
✉ Avenue El Quadissia, Hivernage ☎ 024 44 88 11; www.essaadi.com

Résidence Goumassine (€)
A budget option in the new city. No frills, but decent apartments, studios and some rooms. There is a small pool, bar and breakfast is included.
✉ 71 Boulevard Mohammed Zerktouni, Guéliz ☎ 024 43 30 86; www.residencegoumassine.ma

Sofitel Marrakech (€€–€€€)
If you feel more comfortable with international service and comfort this is a reliable chain hotel with over 300 rooms, just a

15-minute walk to the medina. Ask for a deluxe or superior room when booking as the standard ones can be disappointing.

✉ Rue Harroun Errachid, Hivernage

☎ 024 425 600; www.sofitel.com

Villa Lotus Eva (€€–€€€)

With just five rooms, this place offers the romantic intimacy of a riad, but the quiet and comfort of a hotel outside the medina. All rooms have mini bars, hi-fis and microwaves. Price deals for families and cots are available.

✉ 22 Fbal Zefriti, Hivernage

☎ 024 431 537; www.riadslotus.com

RESTAURANTS

L'Abyssin (€€€)

Where the Beckhams might eat if they were in town. Unashamedly over-the-top restaurant and open-air cocktail bar with beds by the pool. French nouvelle cuisine, but the experience is more memorable than the food.

✉ Km 6, Palais Rhoul Route de Fes, La Palmeraie ☎ 024 328 584; www.restaurant-labyssin.com ⏰ Daily 7pm–late

Le Bagatelle (€€)

Good, traditional French bistro fare has been served at this restaurant since 1949. Feast on well-cooked duck or steak on the delightful terrace.

✉ 101 Rue de Yougoslavie, Guéliz ☎ 024 43 02 74 ⏰ Thu–Tue 12–2:30pm, 7–midnight

Bô-Zin (€€–€€€)

There's a noticeably Thai accent on the food here but you'll find a good selection of Italian and French dishes too. The reason to come here, though, is to dine and dance in the beautiful garden setting. This is arubably one of the best nights out in the city.

✉ Douar Lahna, Km 3.5 Route de l'Ourika ☎ 024 38 80 12; www.bo-zin.com ⏰ Daily 7pm–late

Comptoir Darna (€€€)

Probably the most recommended restaurant in the city, mostly because of its polished performances by belly dancers (at 10:30pm). Insist on a table in the main room. The cooking style is nouvelle cuisine. Reservations essential.

✉ Avenue Echouhada, Hivernage ☎ 024 43 77 02;
www.comptoirdarna.com ⏰ Daily 7pm–late

Kechmara (€–€€)

There isn't a bad time to come here; breakfast (orchid oolong tea, delicious crêpes), lunch of a roast beef sandwich or warm goat's cheese salad and dinner (international, daily changing menu) are all enjoyable. The minimalist interior, smooth music and excellent food always draw the crowds.

✉ 3 Rue de la Liberté, Guéliz ☎ 024 42 25 32;
www.kechmara.com ⏰ Mon–Sat 7am–midnight

Lolo Quoi (€€–€€€)

A stylish, seductive bar and restaurant, where the lighting is low and the food rich (mostly meat and pasta) but consistently good. Try a thick succulent steak the size of your fist with pasta gratin.

✉ 82 Avenue Hassan II ☎ 072 56 98 64 ⏰ Mon–Sat 12:30–3pm, 7–12am

Le Palais Jad Mahal (€€€)

Dining here is like eating in a Parisian palace with Indian-inspired décor. High quality French-Moroccan food, accompanied by belly dancers and a DJ at midnight. Reservations essential.

✉ 10 Rue Haroun Errachid, Hivernage ☎ 024 43 69 84 ⏰ Daily 8am–2am

Restaurant Al Fassia (€€€)

A favourite with locals and visitors alike. Superb, home-cooked food (à la carte Moroccan) served in formal surroundings. A women's cooperative, where the chefs, waiting staff and even the management are all female. Reservations essential.

✉ 55 Boulevard Zerktouni, Guéliz ☎ 024 43 40 60; www.alfassia.com
⏰ Tue–Sun noon–2:30, 7:30–1pm

Rotisserie de la Paix (€€–€€€)

The garden of the Rotisserie of Peace is particularly lovely at night when it is candle lit. Juicy charcoaled meats and winning *plats du jours* of French favourites have been satisfy visitors since 1949.

✉ 68 Rue Yougoslavie, Guéliz ☎ 024 43 31 18 🕐 Tue–Sun 12–2:30, 7:30–11

SHOPPING

Côté Sud

The three levels of this tiny shop are full of contemporary Moroccan delights for the home, such as orange sorbet candles, pretty silk cushion covers and funky coloured tin chandeliers.

✉ 4 Rue de la Liberté, Guéliz ☎ 024 43 84 48 🕐 Mon–Sat 9–12:30, 3:30–7:30

Intensité Nomade

If you are after couture kaftans, or even one in camouflage print, this is the place to come.

✉ 70 Rue de la Liberté, Guéliz ☎ 024 43 13 33
🕐 Mon–Sat 9–1, 3:30–7:30

Michele Baconnier

Original designs and modern takes on Moroccan favourites, including jewellery, lanterns and bags.

✉ 6 Rue du Vieux ☎ 024 44 91 78 🕐 Mon–Sat 9:30–12:30, 3:30–7:30

L'Orientaliste

Beautifully decorated bottles, artisan pieces of pottery, tea glasses and bowls. Reasonable prices; great for gifts.

✉ 15 Rue de la Liberté, Guéliz ☎ 024 43 70 74
🕐 Mon–Sat 9–12:30, 3–7

Place Vendome

Desirable soft leather bags, wallets and jackets, all stylishly designed. Prices, however, would not be out of place in Paris.

✉ 141 Avenue Mohamed V ☎ 024 43 52 63 🕐 Mon–Sat 9–1, 3:30–7:30

Scenes de Lin

Textiles and linens in lovely colours and embroidered cushions are only some of the pretty and practical items on sale here.

✉ 70 Rue de la Liberté, Guéliz ☎ 024 43 61 08

🕐 Mon–Sat 9–1, 3:30–7:30

ENTERTAINMENT

BARS AND NIGHTLIFE

Chesterfield

This smoky 'English pub' has draught beer and shows football on the big screen. The rooftop terrace next to the pool is a nice spot for tea and cocktails and there is also a courtyard garden; avoid the apricot and chintz restaurant.

✉ 115 Avenue Mohamed V ☎ 024 44 64 01 🕐 Daily, hours vary

Coleur Pourpre

One of the newest clubs in the city, but looks set to become a long-standing favourite. Cocktail lounge, tapas, live music, shows, DJ, karaoke – take your pick.

✉ 7 Rue Ibn Zaidoune, Guéliz ☎ 024 43 73 02 🕐 Daily 8pm–2am

Pacha

See page 65.

Theatro

The opulent interior of this former theatre is now a nightclub featuring Ladies', Ministry of Sound and theme nights. Performers fill the large, galleried space and their attempts to make this an 'experience' do work; one of the most enjoyable clubs in Marrakech.

✉ Hotel Es Saadi, Ave El Quadissia ☎ 024 44 88 11; www.theatromarrakech.com 🕐 Daily 11pm–5am

BEACH CLUBS AND SPAS

Nikki Beach

See page 65.

Oasiria Water Park
See page 61.

Palais Rhoul
One of a number of slick new spas offering an exclusive experience. Visit for a massage or one of a range of beauty treatments.

✉ Route de Fes – Dar tounsi ☎ 024 32 94 94;www.palais-rhoul.com
🕐 Daily 9–6

La Plage Rouge
Attracts a mixed crowd who come to drink champagne from red beds around the 70-metre pool. There's also a restaurant and bar with live music.

✉ Km 10, Route de l´Ourika ☎ 024 37 80 86 🕐 Daily 10am–late

SPORT

Dunes & Desert Exploration
These are a thrilling half-day excursion out of the city. Choose between go-karting, quad biking trips and camel rides through a landscape of dried-out rivers, palm trees and Berber villages.

✉ Hôtel Club Palmariva, Km 6, Route de Fès, Marrakech
☎ 061 24 69 48; www.dunesdesert.com

Marrakech Loisirs
Stand-up scooter, camel, horse and calèche rides in the La Palmeraie area can be booked by the hour or longer. More expensive than a taxi but this is a fun way to tour the area.

☎ 061 45 50 34; www.marrakechloisirs.com

Royal Golf Course
Built in 1923, the oldest course in Morocco and superior to the other two 18-hole courses (at the time of writing, several more championship courses were being built). Well maintained, if rather uniform course, where royalty and Churchill have putted.

✉ BP634 Ancienne Route de Ouarzazate ☎ 024 40 47 05 🕐 Daily 7–6

Excursions

When the hustle and bustle of the medina all gets too much, the perfect antidote is within hours of the city. Driving south or east from Marrakech, it is less than an hour before the ascent begins into the Atlas Mountains, a region of soaring peaks and fertile valleys dotted with traditional Berber villages clinging to the hillsides. This accessible landscape, with its evocative kasbahs (mud brick fortresses) attracts casual visitors on day trips, as well as more experienced hill-walkers and climbers looking for extended diversions. Beyond the hills is Ouarzazate, entry point to the Sahara and scene of classic desert movies. A three-hour drive west of Marrakech is the delightful coastal resort of Essaouira, a lovely, laid-back beach destination with all the charms of an ancient town.

Atlas Mountains and the Sahara

AMIZMIZ AND LAKE TAKERKOUST

If you don't have the time or inclination for an extended excursion, but would like a break from the dust and heat of Marrakech, opt for this day trip to a pleasant lake, combined with a visit to the small Berber town of Amizmiz, 55km (34 miles) southwest of Marrakech. Tuesday is the best day when the town's 10,000 population is swollen by village farmers coming in for the weekly market and there is a glimpse of how trade is conducted outside the tourist areas. Lake Takerkoust (15km/9 miles before the town) is a man-made oasis that seems a world away from dusty Marrakech. Dotted around the lake's edge are numerous restaurants and hotels, such as Relais du Lac (➤ 149) that double as activity centres for kayaking, jet-skis, or even horse riding and can supply all the equipment you need. Alternatively, find your own quiet spot for a relaxing dip.

Amizmiz

✉ Km 45, Route S507 (from Marrakech, turn off R203 to Taroudant after 8km/5 miles)

Lake Takerkoust

✉ Km 30, Route S507 (from Marrakech, turn off R203 to Taroudant, after 8km/5 miles) 🍴 Relais du Lac (➤ 149)

ASNI AND IMLIL

Gateway to the Atlas Mountains, the busy little town of Asni, 50km (31 miles) south of Marrakech, is not really a destination in itself, although the Saturday market is a great place to sample the crops produced by local fruit-farmers. Beyond Asni, a rough road leads on to the smaller village of Imlil. On the way is Richard Branson's five-star Kasbah Tamadot (➤ 149) a delicious retreat for the well-heeled. Imlil lies at 1,740m (5,710ft) above sea level and is a good place to stop and acclimatise to the altitude, perhaps with a night or two at Douar Samra (➤ 148). Kasbah du Toubkal (➤ 149) also offers good accommodation and popular day trips from Marrakech called 'A Day with The Berbers'. Many of Imlil's locals work as guides for treks up Jebel Toubkal (➤ 136), touting

for business in the village square-come-bus-stop, while their donkeys provide tourist transport. For the best guides head to the Club Alpin Français (CAF) which is also a cheap place to spend the night. Huge displaced boulders are a common site around both villages, reminders of past flash-flood disasters. The most recent of these in 1995, flattened large parts of the settlements.

Asni

✉ Km 47, R203

Imlil

✉ From Asni, a rough road runs 15km (9 miles) uphill to Imlil 🍴 The village 'shopping centre' has two small cafés ❓ CAF (Club Alpin Français) ☎ 024 31 90 36; www.caf-maroc.com

JEBEL TOUBKAL

The ascent to the summit of North Africa's highest peak (4,167m) is a once-in-a-lifetime opportunity for many people. You don't need to be an experienced climber – just reasonably fit. Go in June to September, after the snow has melted, though you may have to wait for just the right weather. Take a guide and plan on spending the night in the refuge at the 3,200m (10,500ft) snow line, before conquering the summit the next day.

✉ Access to the hiking paths from Imlil (➤ 134) 🍴 Dinner and a bed in the CAF snow-line refuge will cost around 8 euros ☎ 024 31 90 36 ❓ Good guides can be found at the CAF refuge in Imlil (➤ 134), or you can ask for advice in Kasbah du Toubkal (➤ 149). You should plan on paying your guide 20–30 euros per day

OUKAÏMEDENE

On the road to Setti Fetma (➤ 137), take the right turn just before the village of Aghbalou to this ski-resort at 2,650m (8,695ft) above sea level. The journey from Marrakech is 90 minutes and you can hire all the equipment you need once there. It may seem strange to come to Morocco and go skiing, but it's a great day out; the accommodation is not recommended. The queues are always small and the prices much lower than in European or American resorts. For decent snow coverage, visit in January or February.

✉ Km 28, R6035, Toubkal Massif (take the S513 from Marrakech to Setti Fatma)

OURIKA VALLEY

Through the foothills of the Atlas range, flows the Ourika River giving life to this fertile valley. It is a wonderful contrast to the dusty, crowded streets of Marrakech, 40km (25 miles) from the foot of the valley. Berber families have worked the land here in

much the same way for centuries, living in simple clay homes clustered into small hamlets. If time is short, this is a great one-day excursion. A grand taxi from the city into the heart of the valley takes around an hour; you can have a full day's hiking and relaxing by the river, and be back in Marrakech in time for dinner.

Setti Fatma

This growing, mostly modern, riverside village, where many locals have taken to the guide business, is at the end of the paved road from Marrakech into the Ourika Valley. The main attraction is in the hills above the village – a scenic collection of streams, pools and waterfalls. Guides will tell you that it is an easy hike but make sure you wear a pair of sturdy shoes and don't expect to get anywhere quickly, up to the waterfalls takes a couple of hours, although there are easier walks along rough footpaths. The village itself is not particularly attractive, but if you're here in late August, try and catch the *moussem*, which is an all-day festival of music, dance and culture that lasts for three days.

✉ Km 60, Route S513, Ourika Valley 🚍 Communal grand taxis (➤ 28) leave from Marrakech all morning, and return late in the evening 🍴 Good food in Café Asgaour (€) overlooking the river ❓ Guides will charge 15 or 20 euros to take you up to the waterfalls

TAHANOUTE

Less than thirty minutes drive south of Marrakech is this little Berber town on the way to Asni (► 134), best reached by grand taxi from the city. Each Tuesday and Saturday, the market here is alive with farmers, buyers and livestock. It's a chance to see how the locals earn their living and everyone is very friendly, so plan on staying for an informal lunch before heading on or back to Marrakech.

✉ Km 33, R203 Route de Taroudant

TIZI-N-TEST

Historically, control of the Atlas range hinged on a few key *tizis* (mountain passes). In the 1920s, the French cut a new road through this pass, effectively stripping the Berber tribes of their access to the south and control of this mountainous region.

Beyond Asni (► 134), the pass rises over the mountains then rapidly tumbles down to the Sous plains and desert heat of Taroudant, a walled town and Kasbah with souks similar to old Marrakech. Join an organised tour into this mountain pass, or simply hire a grand taxi (► 28), perhaps finishing off with a stay at luxurious La Gazelle D'Or (► 148) in Taroudant.

Ouirgane

The small village of Ouirgane is not too far into the pass and is a good place for an overnight stay before returning to Marrakech or negotiating the hairpin bends of the mountain road beyond. The village is not particularly atractive but is surrounded by pleasant orchards and woods that invite evening strolls and daytime mule treks. Spend the night at Domaine Le Rosarie (► 148), a spa hotel on the edge of the town, or at more basic Dar Tassa (► 148) in the nearby hills. Both hotels will organise excursions to Tin Mal and activities in the countryside.

✉ Km 60, R203 Route de Taroudant

Tin Mal

For a time in the 12th century, Tin Mal was a rear staging post in the Almohads' siege of Marrakech. The mosque here was built in 1153 and shortly afterwards defensive features were added to make the imposing fortress that still overlooks the pass. For non-Muslims, Tin Mal offers a rare chance to step inside a Moroccan mosque, the roof is gone, but much of the structure is well preserved and subject to further restoration. Today, there are just a few houses and an olive press below the mosque. The riverside is a good place for a picnic.

✉ Km 95, R203 Route de Taroudant, halfway from Marrakech to Taroudant

TIZ-N-TICHKA

The N9 highway from Marrakech leads east into this Atlas Mountain pass and for those who suffer from vertigo it feels a lot safer than the Tizi-n-Test. You can easily hire a grand taxi (➤ 28) to take you on a sightseeing day-trip from Marrakech along the length of the pass, ending at Ouarzazate on the edge of the Sahara. Rushing, it is a four-hour drive, but take your time and savour the breathtaking views en route and visit awe-inspiring mountain fortresses at Telouet and Aït Benhaddou. Just 40km (25 miles) from Marrakech, the Berber market at Ait Ourir is in full swing on Tuesdays and Saturdays.

Aït Benhaddou

This red-mud *ksar* (fortified town) is a UNESCO world heritage site, but that has not stopped it crumbling away, so see it while it still stands. It's a labyrinthine and evocatively ancient place, now largely deserted and used primarily as a location for epic desert movies. If you're in a grand taxi, you will need to hike the last few kilometres to the sight, or you can join a 4x4 tour with Berber Tours (➤ 141) in Ouarzazate.

✉ Km170, Route N9 (then 10km (6 miles) on the off-road track to the north) 🕓 Daily, during daylight hours 💷 Free

Kasbah Telouet

This is the former mountain stronghold of the legendary Glaoui brothers, fierce and canny Berber leaders who between them ran large parts of the country for 90 years until 1956. Walking around the medieval maze of buildings, it is hard to believe there was nothing here before the Glaoui, yet perhaps the foreboding feel of the dark ages is

what they were aiming for. Many parts of the complex are sadly closed to visitors, due to the chance of great chunks of adobe crashing down, but what remains is spectacular.

✉ Km 25, Route 6802 (turn off left from N9 at Km109, at the "Ouarzazate 83 km" sign) ☀ Daily, during daylight hours ✋ Small donation suggested for entry

Ouarzazate

The town was created by the French as a key southern outpost guarding the Tiz-n-Tichka. Heavily promoted as 'gateway to the Sahara', what lies immediately beyond Ouarzazate is scrubland, more akin to the Australian bush than the undulating dunes from *Lawrence of Arabia*, parts of which were filmed at nearby Aït Benhaddou. Ouarzazate has fortifications of its own in the form of Kasbah Taourirt, a former home of the Pacha Glaoui dating from the 17th century. Also worth a quick visit while here are the **Atlas Film Studios**, where you can see what's left of sets from epic movies such as *Gladiator* and *Star Wars*. It was hoped that movies like this would generate more interest in Ouarzazate, but today the city's 80,000 residents eke out a simple life when there are no filmmakers in residence. Most visitors are are passing through on their way to desert adventures. **Berber Tours** offer 4x4 excursions to sights around Ouarzazate, as well as camel expeditions into the Sahara from 2 to 15 days.

✉ Km200, Route N9

Atlas Film Studios

☎ 022 54 15 56; www.atlasstudios.com

Berber Tours

☎ 061 43 96 90; www.berbertours.net

Essaouira

The extended N8 motorway from Marrakech makes the 180km (112 mile) drive to Essaouira a breeze, so you can leave after breakfast and be dipping your toes in the ocean before lunchtime. This pretty port town and its beaches attract a mixture of wind surfers, artists, hippies and chilled-out young holidaymakers escaping the dust of Marrakech. Here you can expect the freshest sea food, a rich musical heritage and a relaxed take on the Islamic way of life.

✉ Km100 Route 207, leaving the N8 from Marrakech after 80km (50 miles)

BEACHES

The main beach here, on the south edge of the town, is a wide and sandy playground for locals and tourists alike. Join in a game of football, laze in the hot sun and refreshing, sometimes bracing, *alizeés* (trade winds), or try your hand at windsurfing. If you don't plan a trip to the desert (► 141), why not try a camel ride along the sands here? Negotiating with the camel handlers on the beach is as much an art as souk-haggling – but always offer what you think is reasonable and stay firm to your price. The beach curves south for a kilometre (0.6 miles) to the evocative Borj El Berod, an old fort that has partly crumbled beneath the waves. Walk here when the tide is out to see as much of it as possible, but don't believe the local fairytale about Hendrix being inspired by the Borj to write *Castles Made of Sand* – he did visit, but long after the song was written. For swimming, the northern beach, Plage de Safi, is quieter and calm if the winds are down (try to swim where and when the locals do).

GALERIE DAMGAARD

There are countless small art galleries here and Essaouira has drawn an artistic crowd since the 1950s. They have a vibrant palette to work from – the buildings are bright white, the beaches are golden and the sea is blue. Thrown in the mix is the red of the desert, and the results range from psychedelic abstract to naïve realism. In Damgaard, works across the full spectrum are on sale and display, almost all by local artists.

✉ Ave Oqba Nafiaa ☎ 024 78 44 46; www.galeriedamgaard.com

MEDINA

Essaouira looks older, but it was only built in the 18th century, the brainchild of a Moroccan Sultan who had captured a French architect. The traditional medina and rampart walls are here but within the streets are laid out on a European grid, and the whitewashed buildings dazzle, contrasting beautifully with their azure blue shutters. Stroll the cobbled streets and you will find hidden cafés, restaurants, galleries and craft shops. The exception is at the north end of the medina, in the old Jewish quarter, known as the Mellah, where 40 per cent of the population were squeezed into 10 per cent of the town. Most left after independence and this part of the medina now has a dilapidated feel to it.

MUSÉE DES ARTS ET TRADITIONS POPULAIRE

The small town museum showcases the Essaouira craftsmanship that is famed throughout Morocco. Come here to see the finest examples of marquetry, where veneers are inlaid into wooden items to make fine decorative patterns, before heading to Skala de la Ville where items of the same quality are for sale. The marquetry technique is also used to make Gnawa musicians' string instruments and you will see quite a few on display here, along with pictures of Essaouira from days gone by.

✉ Rue Derb Laalouj ☎ 024 47 23 00 ⏰ Wed–Mon 8:30–12, 2:30–6

PLACE MOULAY HASSAN

This buzzing square which opens down to the harbour is the hub of the town's day and night life. The square is lined with pleasant pavement cafés and it's tempting to spend the whole day here chatting and people-watching. The square is one of the main venues for the huge, fun Gnawa music festival in June (➤ 24). The Gnawa people are descended from sub-Saharan slaves, who as late as 1900 were still sold here. Their religion came to be a mixture of Islam and their own ancient rituals, kept alive today through their music and dance which is rich in symbolism.

SKALA DE LA VILLE

These monumental ramparts guard the western and northern sea
approaches to the harbour, as well as holding back the ocean.
A walk along the top of the ramparts, past the cannons given to
the old Sultan by European powers, affords fantastic views over
the medina and out to the ocean, particularly from the Bab Ljhad
tower at the northern end. Above the ramparts you will find local
artists offering their paintings for sale. Down below, built into
the sea wall are the wood workshops and souks, offering the
finest crafts anywhere in the country and probably at the fairest

prices. Ornate chess sets made from the local Thuya hardwood are easy to carry and if you can get them home, some of the furniture pieces are exquisite.

SKALA DU PORT

The port is the place to come at around 3pm when the fishing boats are heading in to drop their catch. The whole place comes alive and for two hours is filled with auctioneers, fisherman and buyers, as well as curious visitors. Sardines, lobsters and crabs are unloaded and rapidly sold and the catch finds its way to the open-air grill stands that stand between the port and Place Moulay Hassan. Alfresco dining at its best, dishes are concocted in a matter of minutes and eaten on the spot. If you want to get out onto the ocean, you can hire a boat in the morning and catch your own fish to be grilled in the port.

HOTELS

ATLAS MOUNTAINS AND THE SAHARA

Beldi Country Club (€€)

Built as a *douar* (Moroccan hamlet), with gardens, terraces and a lake-like pool surrounded by olive and palm trees. Excellent cuisine.

✉ Km 6, Route du Barrage, Cherifia ☎ 024 38 39 50; www.beldicountryclub.com

Dar Tassa (€)

The two attractions here are the welcoming atmosphere and the panoramic views of Toubkal Park. An excellent-value Berber guesthouse, with friendly mountain guides. Consider an overnight stay and a day trek with transport provided from Marrakech.

✉ Douar Tassa, ✉ P176, Ouirgane ☎ 079 88 60 81; www.dartassa.com

Domaine Le Rosarie (€–€€)

A lovely spot near the Tizi-n-Test pass. Visit for the spectacular gardens surrounded by the High Atlas Mountains, relaxing by the pool and horse riding, which will compensate for the rather bland rooms and down-at-heel spa services.

✉ Km 60, Route de Taroudant, Ouirgane ☎ 024 48 56 93; www.laroseraiehotel.com

Douar Samra (€)

Arrive by donkey from Imlil at this rustic trekking base in the hamlet of Tamartet, close to the summits of the Atlas Mountains. Rooms are basic with intermittent hot water, but pretty with real fires and the hospitality is second to none. Full or half board.

✉ 1.6km (1 mile) from Imlill ☎ 024 37 86 05; www.douar-samra.com

La Gazelle D'Or (€€€)

Despite the prices, don't expect five-star luxury; think local and Berber, with picnics and trekking. Modern, spacious interiors, although some rooms have seen better days. Dinner can be served around the pool or in a private pavilion. There are 200 acres of gardens with orange groves.

✉ Route d'Amezgrou, Taroudant ☎ 028 85 20 48; www.gazelledor.com

Kasbah du Toubkal (€–€€€)

Accommodation from dorms to suites in a restored kasbah, just beyond the village of Imlil. Popular for day trips which include a visit to Imlil, the Kasbah for lunch and a Berber village. Can also arrange longer packages, and works closely with the local community – 5 per cent of hotel bills goes back to the villages.

✉ BP 31, Imlil ☎ 01883 744392; www.kasbahdutoubkal.com

Kasbah Tamadot (€€€)

'Sir Richard Branson's Moroccan retreat' is in a spectacular location. It's the only option in the area if you want faultless European food and service, although it is rather corporate and impersonal. The 18 rooms are filled with antiques, there's an infinity pool and not surprisingly, a hot-air balloon.

✉ BP 67, Asni ☎ 024 36 82 00; www.kasbahtamadot.virgin.com

Relais du Lac (€)

Basic but pleasant lakeside villa, where you can stop for lunch or dinner, or spend a night or two with canoe trips on the lake and hikes around the shore. The rooms are functional, but the food is tasty and good value. For a fun evening, you can spend the night in a Bedouin tent by the lake.

✉ Relais du Lac, BP 44 Route d'Azizmizmiz, C/R Lalla takerkoust
☎ 024 48 49 24 /061 18 74 72; www.aubergedulac-marrakech.com

Berber Palace (€€€)

On the expensive side, but this is five-star luxury with well equipped rooms. The charming pool offers welcome relief from the heat, and there are a host of activities to chose from, including desert 4x4 trips.

✉ Quartier Mansour Eddahbi, Ouarzazate ☎ 024 88 31 05;
www.ouarzazate.com

ESSAOUIRA

L'Heure Bleue (€€€)

This 200-year-old riad may be a palace but the service and intermittent air conditioning can be disappointing. Breakfast with the birds in the courtyard and have dinner in the Relais & Chateaux restaurant. Spa, library and cinema.

✉ 2 Rue Ibn Batouta ☎ 024 78 34 34; www.heure-bleue.com

Madada Mogador (€)

Small but stylish and a bit of a gem, with just seven spacious rooms. Panoramic views from the terrace looking out to sea. Friendly and efficient staff, delicious breakfasts and Wi-Fi.

✉ 5 Rue Youssef El Fassi ☎ 024 47 55 12; www.madada.com

Riad de la Mer (€)

Welcoming, charming 18th-century riad furnished with antiques. In a wonderful location with views of both the town and the sea from the terrace. Communal kitchen. The whole house can be rented and sleeps nine.

☎ 060 75 58 94; www.riaddelamer.co.uk

Riad Lotus O Marine (€€–€€€)

All five rooms in this riad offer contemporary luxury: minibar, Hi-fi and DVD player. Named after famous people, pick one according to your muse, whether Onassis, Dali or Fellini. This Riad also has a traditional hammam and a terrace.

✉ 22 Fbal Zefriti Quartier Ksour (head office in Marrakech)
☎ 024 43 15 37; www.riadslotus.com

RESTAURANTS

Les Alizés (€€–€€€)

Perhaps the most popular place in town. Simple, intimate restaurant with relaxed atmosphere and excellent, traditional Moroccan cuisine.

✉ 26 Rue de la Skala, Essaouira ☎ 024 47 68 19 ⏰ Daily 7–11pm

Le Chalet de la Plage (€€)

The beachfront location is the main attraction of this long-standing restaurant; visit for a snack, seafood or pasta and drink in the view. It is popular so advance reservation is advised.

✉ 1 Boulevard Mohamed V, Essaouira ☎ 024 47 59 72 ⏰ Tue–Sun 9am–11pm; closed Sun lunchtime

Le Cinq (€€–€€€)

Part of the Madada Mogador hotel, this is a contemporary restaurant with bright décor and modern Italian and French cuisine. Wi-fi and occasional live music.

✉ 7 Rue Youssef El Fassi, Essaouira ☎ 024 78 47 26 ⏰ 12am–12pm, closed Tuesdays

Fresh fish stalls (€–€€€)

At lunchtime, get the daily catch of your choice, from sardines to lobster. Prices are per kilo (but watch for overcharging) and the fish is cooked in front of you for the freshest lunch possible.

✉ Entrance to the harbour, Essaouira ☎ No phone ⏰ Daily

ENTERTAINMENT

Bar Taros

In a popular spot on the main square, this trendy rooftop café is a good place to hang out in the evenings. Good for cocktails and tapas and there is entertaining live music on some evenings; call in to find out when.

✉ 2 Rue du Skala, Essaouira ☎ 024 47 64 07 ⏰ Mon–Fri 8am–11pm

Ocean Vagabond

Windsurfing, surfing and kite surfing, with or without an instructor, as well as the less serene and environmentally friendly quad biking are all available from this nautical centre on the beach. All equipment is supplied for hire.

✉ Boulevard Mohamed V, Essaouira ☎ 024 78 39 34; www.oceanvagabond.com

Index

Street index

Acknowledgements

The Automobile Association wishes to thank the following photographers, companies and picture libraries for their assistance in the preparation of this book.

Abbreviations for the picture credits are as follows – (t) top; (b) bottom; (l) left; (r) right; (c) centre; (AA) AA World Travel Library; (IFC) Inside Front Cover.

4l Koutoubia Mosque at night, AA/S McBride; **4c** Boulevard Yamouk, Marrakech, AA/A Mockford and N Bonetti; **4r** Koutoubia Gardens and Mosque, AA/A Mockford and N Bonetti; **5l** Atlas Mountains, AA/S McBride; **5c** Agdal Gardens, AA/A Mockford and N Bonetti; **5r** Skala de la Ville, AA/A Mockford and N Bonetti; **6/7** Koutoubia Mosque at night, AA/S McBride; **8/9** Berber musicians, Essaouira, AA/A Mockford and N Bonetti; **10** View from Skala de la Ville, Essaouira, AA/A Mockford and N Bonetti; **11tl** Jemaa El Fna, Marrakech, AA/A Mockford and N Bonetti; **11tr** Bab Debbagh, Marrakech, AA/A Mockford and N Bonetti; **12** Jemaa El Fna, stall, AA/A Mockford and N Bonetti; **12/13t** Tagines cooking in street, Marrakech, AA/A Mockford and N Bonetti; **12/13c** Dried fruit stall, Jemaa El Fna, AA/A Mockford and N Bonetti; **13t** Seafood *briousettes*, Essaouira, AA/A Mockford and N Bonetti; **13c** Olive and pickle stall, Central Market, AA/A Mockford and N Bonetti; **14** Moroccan salad, Essaouira, AA/A Mockford and N Bonetti; **14/15** Biscuits for sale, Marrakech, AA/A Mockford and N Bonetti; **15** Teapot and tea glasses, Dar Papillon, Essaouira, AA/A Mockford and N Bonetti; **16c** Koutoubia Mosque, AA/A Mockford and N Bonetti; **16b** Jemaa El Fna, Mosque Minaret, AA/A Mockford and N Bonetti; **17** Rue Souk Smarine, AA/A Mockford and N Bonetti; **18t** Ait Benhaddou, Berber guide, AA/A Mockford and N Bonetti; **18b** Badii Palace, Marrakech, AA/A Mockford and N Bonetti; **18/19t** Beach, Essaouira, AA/A Mockford and N Bonetti; **18/19b** Ait Benhaddou, AA/A Mockford and N Bonetti; **19** Ben Youssef Medersa sign, AA/A Mockford and N Bonetti; **20/21** Traffic Boulevard Yamouk, Marrakech, AA/A Mockford and N Bonetti; **25** Festival of Berber Tribe, Photolibrary Group; **27** Road signs, Marrakech, AA/A Mockford and N Bonetti; **28** Grand taxi, Marrakech, AA/A Mockford and N Bonetti; **31** Post box, Marrakech, AA/A Mockford and N Bonetti; **34/35** Koutoubia Mosque from gardens, AA/A Mockford and N Bonetti; **36** City Walls, Boulevard Yarmouk, Marrakech, AA/A Mockford and N Bonetti; **36/37** Seven Saints Gate, Marrakech, AA/A Mockford and N Bonetti; **38/39** Museum of Islamic Arts, AA/A Mockford and N Bonetti; **39** Museum of Islamic Arts, AA/A Mockford and N Bonetti; **40** Ménara Gardens, view across the basin, AA/A Mockford and N Bonetti; **40/41** Ménara Gardens, view to High Atlas, AA/A Mockford and N Bonetti; **41** Ménara Gardens, view to High Atlas, AA/A Mockford and N Bonetti; **42** Koutoubia Mosque, AA/A Mockford and N Bonetti; **42/43t** Koutoubia Mosque minaret, AA/A Mockford and N Bonetti; **42/43b** Tomb of Fatima Zohra, AA/A Mockford and N Bonetti; **44** Ben Youssef Medersa, courtyard, AA/A Mockford and N Bonetti; **45t** Ben Youssef Medersa, tile decoration, AA/A Mockford and N Bonetti; **45b** Central Courtyard, Ben Youssef Medersa, AA/A Mockford and N Bonetti; **46** Marrakech Museum, AA/A Mockford and N Bonetti; **46/47** Marrakech Museum, Inner central courtyard, AA/A Mockford and N Bonetti; **47** Door detail Marrakech Museum, AA/A Mockford and N Bonetti; **48/49** Jemaa El Fna at night, AA/A Mockford and N Bonetti; **49** Foodstall, Jemaa El Fna at night, AA/A Mockford and N Bonetti; **50** Badii Palace, Marrakech, AA/A Mockford and N Bonetti; **50/51** Badii Palace, Marrakech, AA/A Mockford and N Bonetti; **51** Badii Palace, Marrakech, AA/A Mockford and N Bonetti; **52/53t** Souk La Criee Berbere, AA/A Mockford and N Bonetti; **52/53b** Souk Talaa, Marrakech, AA/A Mockford and N Bonetti; **53** Rue Riad Zitoun El Kedim, AA/A Mockford and N Bonetti; **54** Mausoleum of Ahmed al-Mansour, Saâdian Tombs, AA/A Mockford and N Bonetti; **55** El Mansour's tomb, Saâdian Tombs, AA/A Mockford and N Bonetti; **56/57** Atlas Mountains, AA/S McBride; **58** Café Poste, Ave Mohammed V, AA/A Mockford and N Bonetti; **58/59** Place

Sight locator index

This index relates to the maps on the covers. We have given map references to the main sights in the book.

Dear Reader

**Your comments, opinions and recommendations are very important
to us. So please help us to improve our travel guides by taking a few
minutes to complete this simple questionnaire.**

*You do not need a stamp (unless posted outside the UK). If you do not want to cut this page
from your guide, then photocopy it or write your answers on a plain sheet of paper.*

Send to: **The Editor, AA World Travel Guides,
FREEPOST SCE 4598, Basingstoke RG21 4GY.**

Your recommendations...

We always encourage readers' recommendations for restaurants, nightlife or shopping – if
your recommendation is used in the next edition of the guide, we will send you a **FREE AA
Guide** of your choice from this series. Please state below the establishment name, location
and your reasons for recommending it.

_____
_____
_____
_____
_____
_____

Please send me **AA Guide** _____

About this guide...

Which title did you buy?
   AA _____
Where did you buy it? _____
When? **m m / y y**
Why did you choose this guide?_____
_____
_____
_____
_____

Did this guide meet your expectations?
Exceeded ☐   Met all ☐   Met most ☐   Fell below ☐
Were there any aspects of this guide that you particularly liked? _____
_____
_____
_____

continued on next page...

Is there anything we could have done better? _____

_____

_____

About you...

Name (*Mr/Mrs/Ms*)? _____

Address _____

_____

_____ Postcode _____

Daytime tel nos _____

Email _____

Please only give us your mobile phone number or email if you wish to hear from us about other products and services from the AA and partners by text or mms, or email.

Which age group are you in?
Under 25 ☐   25–34 ☐   35–44 ☐   45–54 ☐   55–64 ☐   65+ ☐

How many trips do you make a year?
Less than one ☐   One ☐   Two ☐   Three or more ☐

Are you an AA member? Yes ☐   No ☐

About your trip...

When did you book? m m / y y   When did you travel? m m / y y

How long did you stay? _____

Was it for business or leisure? _____

Did you buy any other travel guides for your trip? _____

If yes, which ones? _____

_____

_____

Thank you for taking the time to complete this questionnaire. Please send it to us as soon as possible, and remember, you do not need a stamp (*unless posted outside the UK*).

> **AA** Travel Insurance call 0800 072 4168 or visit www.theAA.com